Anticompetitive
Practices in Japan

Anticompetitive Practices in Japan

Their Impact on the Performance of Foreign Firms

Masaaki Kotabe
Kent W. Wheiler

Westport, Connecticut
London

Library of Congress Cataloging-in-Publication Data

Kotabe, Masaaki.
   Anticompetitive practices in Japan : their impact on the
performance of foreign firms / Masaaki Kotabe, Kent W. Wheiler.
      p.   cm.
   Includes bibliographical references and index.
   ISBN 0-275-95628-8 (alk. paper)
   1. Restraint of trade—Japan.   2. Industrial policy—Japan.
3. Competition—Japan.   4. Corporations, Foreign—Japan.
5. Protectionism—Japan.   I. Wheiler, Kent W.   II. Title.
HD3616.J32K67   1996
338.6′048′0952—dc20   96-4847

British Library Cataloguing in Publication Data is available.

Library of Congress Catalog Card Number: 96-4847
ISBN: 0-275-95628-8

First published in 1996

Praeger Publishers, 88 Post Road West, Westport, CT 06881
An imprint of Greenwood Publishing Group, Inc.

Printed in the United States of America

The paper used in this book complies with the
Permanent Paper Standard issued by the National
Information Standards Organization (Z39.48–1984).

10 9 8 7 6 5 4 3 2 1

Contents

Contents

Figures

Tables

Episodes

Preface

The U.S.-Japan bilateral trade relationship is perhaps the most consequential, and the most tumultuous, in the world. Government and business leaders devote substantial time and effort to carefully resolving the apparently infinite stream of disputes that arise between these two allies and trading partners. Many of the issues are rooted in a perception that Japan's impressive economic success may be due in some degree to anticompetitive practices through which Japan's domestic markets are protected and an unfair advantage is granted to Japanese companies as they expand abroad. Regardless of the validity of these opinions, their existence exerts a negative influence upon this critically important bilateral relationship between the United States and Japan.

This study examines Japan's pattern of international commerce and the basis for American accusations of unfair trade. A major unsettled question is whether unfair trade practices, if they exist, have a negative impact on the performance of American firms marketing manufactured products in Japan. Three general and overlapping areas of alleged trade barriers are reviewed: government policies and practices, exclusionary *keiretsu* relationships, and anticompetitive behavior. The latter category is examined in greater depth, with particular focus on sensitive issues surrounding the U.S. and Japanese antitrust laws and the behavior that those laws proscribe.

There are many aggregate econometric studies published in research books on this topic. However, they are filled with statistical analyses and econometric modeling and are not widely read by business researchers and practitioners. Furthermore, these research books fail to provide normative guidelines (that is, suggestions as to what foreign businesses should do). On the other hand, there are also a good number of books on characteristics of Japanese business and the Japanese business environment. However, they tend to describe either unique Japanese business practices and aspects of the environment or anecdotal cases. None of them squarely deals with Japanese firms' antimonopolistic behavior and its impact on foreign firms' market performance.

Specifically, our study attempts to answer two critical questions relative to the occurrence of anticompetitive behavior in Japan: (1) Does anticompetitive behavior occur more frequently in Japan than in the United States? and if so, (2) Does the occurrence of anticompetitive behavior in Japan have a negative impact on the performance of American companies marketing manufactured goods in Japan? In this research we go beyond what has been investigated previously in the literature by investigating specific anticompetitive acts rather than inquiring about barriers in general. The occurrence of specific anticompetitive behaviors in Japan has not been directly examined earlier due to the sensitive and possibly illegal nature of such practices.

In this study, a research instrument was developed to facilitate the collection of data without requiring the disclosure of potentially incriminating information. The Japan operations of almost 200 large U.S. multinational corporations were included in this study. The findings are clear and surprising: American business executives working and residing in Japan believe that anticompetitive behavior occurs more frequently in Japan than it does in the United States. Japanese executives of U.S. companies do not agree, claiming that there is little difference in the anticompetitive climates of the two countries. Yet despite these contrary opinions, the executives do agree that anticompetitive behavior has not had a negative influence on their business performance, although they seem to foresee the potential for adverse consequences in the future.

This study promises to provide academic rigor as well as relevance to a timely topic, since an increasing number of foreign firms have begun to realize that they can no longer ignore potentially lucrative Japanese markets. The study results provide implications, for U.S. businesses attempting to enter or build their businesses in Japan, as well as U.S. and Japanese government policy makers, trade negotiators, and law enforcement officials.

There are many people who assisted us throughout the course of this time-consuming research project. We are most grateful to William E. Franklin, President of Weyerhaeuser Far East, for his considerable support and assistance. Kumiko Suzuki visited the Tokyo office of the Japan Fair Trade Commission on several occasions, gathering information that helped us understand the enforcement of Japan's antimonopoly law. Jack Hellman, Motoko Nagamatsu, and Azusa Takeda assisted with the data collection. We express our sincere appreciation to the many business executives in Japan who took the time to respond to the questionnaire and to share their experiences and observations with us. We also thank Marcy Weiner and Jim Ice of Greenwood Publishing Group for their persistent encouragement on this project. Marcy persuaded us to write this book, and Jim pushed us to complete it in a timely fashion.

Finally, much love and gratitude are due to Kay and Karen, our comrades in arms. Without their constant encouragement and enormous patience, punctuated with the cheers of our children, this project never would have materialized.

Masaaki Kotabe
University of Texas at Austin
Austin, Texas

Kent W. Wheiler
Weyerhauser
Longview, Washington

1

Anticompetitive Behavior or Not: An Unsettling Issue

Americans trade more goods with Japan than with any other country outside North America. The total volume of U.S.-Japan trade comprises the second largest bilateral trading relationship in the world, exceeded only by the exchange of goods between the United States and Canada. Japan imports more from the United States than from any other country, and is second only to Canada as the largest consumer of products that are made in America. The United States is the largest market for Japanese goods, consuming nearly one-third of Japan's total exports.

Ironically, no trading partner of the United States has been the subject of more frequent and acrimonious trade disputes and negotiations than has Japan. This is not simply a function of the high volume of trade, for Canada is America's largest trading partner but has been involved in only a small fraction of the trade problems Americans face with Japan (Stern 1989). The disputes arise, in part, because the total trade flow is consistently and enormously lopsided in Japan's favor. The United States has incurred a trade deficit with Japan every single year since 1965 (see Figure 1.1).

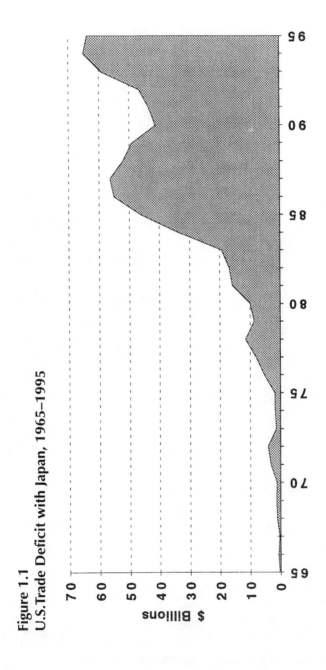

Figure 1.1
U.S. Trade Deficit with Japan, 1965–1995

The trade imbalance alone, however, is insufficient to explain the friction between the United States and Japan. Germany's trade surplus has on occasion been a higher percentage of its GNP than has Japan's, but because Germany is perceived to be a relatively open market, the Germans have avoided many of the trade troubles that plague Japan (Lawrence 1991b, Lincoln 1990). Canada has a consistent and sizable trade surplus with the United States, yet trade disputes are comparatively minor because of the general belief that American and Canadian companies are allowed to trade, invest, and otherwise conduct business across their shared border on equitable terms. In fact, economists claim that there is not necessarily a relationship between the size of a nation's trade surplus and the openness of its markets. Over and above the trade statistics, America's friction with Japan is largely centered around the notion that Japan takes unfair advantage of the free trade system by competing fully in the United States without granting equal access for U.S. companies to operate in Japan. It is this perceived lack of reciprocity, this image of Japan as a closed market, that is the crux of the matter and the premise for the persistent complaints about Japan's trade practices (Cline 1983). Lincoln (1990) aptly summarizes the situation:

> Implicit in the thicket of positions and verbiage is a belief that success by Japanese corporations or industries . . . is acceptable so long as it is truly the product of the sort of economic factors claimed by the Japanese. The problems, then, stem from the conviction that in many cases market outcomes are shaped by Japanese business practices considered unfair— predatory pricing, patent infringement, industrial espionage, and explicit or implicit protection of Japanese markets from import competition. . . . This is the basis on which the problem must rest: Japanese success in blocking imports into their own country or in penetrating U.S. markets comes, at least in part, from anticompetitive behavior rather than from competitive ability (pp. 5–6).

It is important to Japan and the United States, and to the world economy, that the issues surrounding Japan's trade behavior and alleged barriers be investigated, understood, and resolved.

Regardless of whether such beliefs are accurate, the important thing is that they exist. The perception that Japan cheats in the marketplace damages not only Japan's long-term credibility and standing abroad but also the fabric of a free trade system upon which Japan so heavily depends (Toyama, Tateishi, and Palenberg 1983, p. 609).

Recognizing that it is the perceptions of political and business leaders, not necessarily reality, that influence government policy and industrial behavior, it is unfortunate that such wide differences continue to exist as to what various opinion leaders believe about trade with Japan. "The evidence is overwhelming," writes Laura Tyson, Berkeley professor and head of President Clinton's Council of Economic Advisors, "that competition [in Japan] is bounded and orchestrated . . . market outcomes are certainly different because such mechanisms for collaboration, collusion, and bargains exist" (Tyson and Zysman 1989, p. 77). On the other hand, Paul Krugman, MIT professor and former member of President Bush's Council of Economic Advisors, claims:

> Does Japan take unfair advantage of our open market while closing its own? Many, perhaps most, Americans believe this, though few economists would agree. . . . The perception of Japan as a villain is at least 95% wrong. Even a brief review of the evidence explodes most of the myths that continue to circulate in U.S. discussion. While there is room to criticize Japan, the idea that Japan is pursuing beggar-my-neighbor policies on a grand scale is essentially preposterous. Nevertheless, many influential Americans believe it (Krugman 1987a, p. 16).

ALLEGATIONS OF UNFAIR TRADE

Accusations, complaints, and reports of Japan's "renegade" behavior are well documented and widely distributed (e.g., Choate 1990, Fallows 1993, Johnson 1982, Pickens 1991, Prestowitz 1988a, 1988b, 1992, Shimaguchi and Lazer 1979). U.S. trade officials recently complained that despite more than 30 bilateral trade agreements since 1980, Japan remains less open to imports than any other industrialized nation (*Nikkei Weekly* 1994b; see also American Chamber of Commerce in Japan 1991, Green and Larsen

1987). An annual report published by the office of the U.S. Trade Representative singled out Japan as the most offensive perpetrator of barriers to competition among all countries accused of unfair trade practices (*Wall Street Journal* 1993a). Brouthers and Werner (1990) applied Porter's (1985) fifteen criteria of a good competitor to the Japanese and concluded that it is "obvious that the Japanese can be clearly considered bad competitors" (p. 9). (Porter defined bad competitors as those that destabilize an industry and/or encourage costly protracted warfare.) President Clinton declared that Japan has bloated its trade surplus by rejecting the promotion of imports and refusing to grant market access in main industries (*Daily Yomiuri* 1994a). Other high-profile government, academic, and business leaders make similar statements: "Many Japanese markets remain closed to products from the United States" (Christopher 1994, p. 361); "Foreign firms are handicapped in their ability to export goods to or invest in their Japanese competitors' home market" (Nye 1992, p. 105); "Japan is a mercantile power, not a free trader" (Johnson 1990b, p. 108); and "Japan has no use for free trade. It certainly has never practiced free trade" (Iacocca 1992, p. 296). Poll takers find that two-thirds of Americans believe Japan unfairly restricts sales of U.S. goods (Smith 1990). The following letter to the editor of the *Wall Street Journal* (1990) from Charles Plushnick of Brooklyn is not atypical of American attitudes toward Japan:

> Your article about the poor mom-and-pop toy stores in Japan threatened with extinction by Toys "R" Us fails to gain much sympathy from me. I would like to know how many articles were written in Japan in the early 1970s about the devastation of Flint, Michigan by the onslaught of Japanese cars. . . . I don't recall the Japanese having much sympathy for America when they ravaged the American consumer-electronics industry, or steel industry, or motorcycle industry, or machine-tool industry, or semiconductor industry. The Japanese claimed that they did not dump their goods into the U.S., that our problems are our own fault and that we don't motivate our workers to adapt to the market or innovate. I agree that Americans are not free of all blame for our trade deficit. But Japan is no longer a backward Third World nation and thus no longer needs protection from foreign competition.

Americans have been perhaps the most active and vocal critics of Japan's competitive methods, but Japan's neighbors in Asia, and the Europeans, have voiced many of the same complaints. Since 1981, Japan has maintained a trade surplus in manufactured products with all of its trading partners, something that "no version of the theory of comparative advantage can account for" (Johnson 1990b, p. 107). South Korea and Taiwan have argued with Japan for many years over nontariff barriers against their products. The European Community (EC) has accused Japan of using profits from high prices in its domestic market to subsidize lower-priced exports to the EC (*Daily Yomiuri* 1992a). In a speech delivered in Japan, the president of the German conglomerate Hoechst's Japan subsidiary declared, "Formal barriers to foreign entry have all but disappeared in Japan, but the real barriers today are in the minds of many business leaders and government bureaucrats who do not truly welcome free competition from anywhere in the world" (Waesche 1993, p. 11). In early 1994, German businessmen residing in Japan reportedly persuaded their government to replace the German ambassador to Japan because he was not tough enough opening up the Japanese market. A former British ambassador to Japan wrote:

> It is true that Japanese barriers have come down and that not all foreign firms have always tried hard enough to penetrate the Japanese market, but Japanese attempts to always lay the blame on foreign firms are at best exaggerated and generally disingenuous. The fact is that many Japanese ministries have demonstrated a singular ability to put obstacles in the way of foreign firms when some of their Japanese clients might be damaged by foreign competition (*Nikkei Weekly* 1994a).

All too often, these complaints and cries of unfairness are arbitrarily dismissed because of their anecdotal nature. While few people would deny the need for careful empirical investigation before conclusions are reached and policy enacted, the consistency, frequency, and prevalence of foreign accusations regarding barriers to trade in Japan certainly justify a healthy skepticism. As one writer put it, "It is somewhat disconcerting to have everyday businessmen's problems of the past thirty years treated as aberrational oddities. These horror stories have been too common and important to handle simply by shrinking them down to the status of anecdotal trash to be swept under the rug" (Henderson 1986, p. 135).

In recent years there has developed a distinction between characterizing Japan's behavior as "different" rather than the more subjective label of "unfair." Largely the product of what has become known as the revisionist school of thought (Fallows 1989, Johnson 1990b, Neff 1989, Prestowitz 1988a, 1998b, van Wolferen 1989, Yamamura 1990), it starts with the premise that Japan's form of capitalism is fundamentally different from other industrialized economies. For example, Japan has emphasized production and industrial welfare, while other countries, most notably the United States, have focused on consumption and consumer welfare; neither approach is inherently "wrong" or "unfair," and both have brought spectacular economic growth and prosperity to their practitioners.

The idea of a "different" Japan has found a receptive audience. Some Japanese scholars have since described their country as a "noncapitalist market economy," practicing "network capitalism" (Nakatani 1992, Sakakibara 1992). But the revisionists face strong resistance when they take the next step and suggest that because Japan is different, it must be treated differently. Their conclusion is that free trade, as defined and practiced by other developed countries, will not work with Japan. Instead, some type of results-oriented, managed trade is required. The Clinton administration has clearly and aggressively adopted this approach, and Japan's government has just as clearly and aggressively rejected it, arguing that as a country committed to the principles of free trade, it cannot consent to any attempt to manage trade.

ASSERTIONS OF FAIR TRADE

Japanese business and government officials, joined by many foreign business leaders and academics, usually respond to accusations of barriers and unfair trade with contrary stories and statistics that demonstrate Japan's openness to imports. The successes of Amway, Coca Cola, IBM, and McDonald's, among others, are cited as proof that U.S. companies can succeed in Japan if they offer a quality product and put forth the effort required. The chairman of Fujitsu, Takuma Yamamoto, laments, "We have to go out of our way to find American products worth buying" (Helms

1991). The chairman of the Japan Paper Association, Jiro Kawake, explains, "High quality in the United States is not necessarily high quality in Japan," and Jiro Furumoto, president of Asahi Glass, complains, "It seems to me that U.S. companies that don't make a sales effort are just trying to give a false impression of their failure" (*Daily Yomiuri* 1991). After reviewing several articles by Japanese authors containing what he terms "the mainstream view in Japan," Lincoln (1990) summarizes their position as follows:

> Many Japanese . . . believe that Japan's markets are as open as those of other countries, that any remaining problems are due to the failure of foreign firms to understand their market, and that the central issues are macroeconomic (p. 13).

On a per capita basis, the average Japanese citizen buys more U.S. products than U.S. citizens buy Japanese products (Kuriyama 1994). Since 1974 (with a few narrow exceptions), Japan has been the world's third largest importer. Japan imports more from America than do West Germany, France, and Italy combined (*Japan Times* 1990). And Japan's average tariff on industrial products is lower than either America's or the EC's.

The manner of tabulating trade statistics and their accurate portrayal of economic realities is often questioned. The United States maintains a large surplus in services trade with Japan, which, if included with the merchandise trade numbers, would reduce the imbalance significantly (*Wall Street Journal* 1993b). Others claim that current trade figures do not account for disparities arising from varying degrees of foreign investment, and that if offshore production of U.S. companies were included, one would find that the Japanese buy an equal amount from American companies as Americans buy from Japanese companies (Totten 1992).

Since 1985, the value of the yen has tripled relative to the dollar, a dramatic change engineered by the United States as a remedy for the trade imbalance, but with results and long-term effects that are controversial. As expected, the stronger yen has led Japan to import more than twice the 1985 volume of manufactured goods. Yet Japanese companies did not stand idly by and watch exchange rates put them out of the export business. They cut costs with a vengeance in order to remain competitive, maintaining quality while developing more efficient, productive operations. And by pushing up the value of Japan's currency, America in effect put U.S. assets on sale for one-half to two-thirds off the original price. As would any astute buyer, Japan came shopping. More than 90 percent of all Japanese direct investment in the United States occurred within the past ten years. Japanese businesses acquired American companies, erected new factories, and expanded their distribution and retail infrastructure to facilitate access to American consumers. Japan's investments in the United States pulled more imports from the motherland because, regardless of nationality, newly established foreign subsidiaries tend to depend more on their parent company for components and equipment (Davidson 1980, Graham and Krugman 1989, Kotabe 1992). Meanwhile on the opposite side of the ocean, Americans saw the already high price of Japan's assets triple. Acquiring established companies, buying land, building factories, and setting up distribution and retail chains to reach Japanese consumers became economically difficult for even the largest and wealthiest U.S. firms.

Keidanren, Japan's influential business lobby, expressed its hope that the United States would "face up to the fact that the trade imbalance with Japan is fundamentally rooted in macroeconomic factors" (Keidanren 1990a, p. 2). There is a preponderance of evidence and opinion supporting this contention. It is a fundamental macroeconomic equation that any country's trade balance will be equal to the sum of domestic savings and tax revenues minus investment and government spending. As long as the United States saves less than it spends and incurs a fiscal deficit, a global trade imbalance will result. If U.S. trade were somehow balanced with Japan but the U.S. fiscal deficit remained, America's trade imbalance would simply shift to another of its trading partners.

Finally, as noted earlier, Japan's trade surplus does not necessarily imply the existence of market barriers. Bhagwati (1994) labels the notion that the trade imbalance is proof that Japan's markets are closed as an "egregious fallacy," and he disdainfully asserts that

> Occasionally, counterintuitive economic sense will prevail for a moment, but then fallacy, so compelling to the untrained mind, resurfaces. Convincing Washington that bilateral surpluses are no index of the openness of markets is as difficult as convincing a peasant that the earth is round when it appears flat to the naked eye (p. 11).

The literature reviewed in Chapter 2 of this work confers some validity on these points of view. Trade barriers are not the predominant cause of the trade gap, and their reduction may not result in a substantial change in the bilateral imbalance. On the other hand, this does not preclude the existence of trade barriers. As Chapter 2 will also show, other researchers have put forth considerable evidence that barriers to imports of manufactured products do exist in Japan. Claims that Japan is different, that Japan acts as a mercantilistic power focused on exports and determined to restrict imports, are not without foundation. Frustrated by the dogmatic belief that since Japan is economically successful it must be practicing free trade, Johnson (1990) decries "the influence of a set of theological principles—the doctrine of free trade—serviced by an entrenched priesthood—the professional economists—that is much more interested in defending its articles of faith than in understanding what is going on in international economic relations" (p. 107). He ironically quotes the father of free trade, Adam Smith, to emphasize his point: "The learned give up the evidence of their senses to preserve the coherence of the ideas of their imagination" (p. 107).

An example of the different views and opinions regarding the openness of a market in Japan is provided in episode 1. See if the reader can easily conclude whether this particular Japanese market is closed or open.

Episode 1.1
Closed Market or Open Market?—The Flat Glass Industry Case

When U.S. Trade Representative Carla Hills visited Japan in November 1991, she urged Japan to open its glass market to imports. The U.S. claims that Japan's ¥300 billion sheet glass market is dominated by three firms—Asahi Glass, Nippon Sheet Glass, and Central Glass—and that they are blocking U.S. sales through their *keiretsu* relationships with wholesalers.

Jiro Furumoto, president of Asahi Glass, expressed surprise at the U.S. demands. "Honestly, I am confused. Our doors are not closed. It seems to me that U.S. companies that do not make a sales effort are just trying to give a false impression of their failure." He believes the market situation in Japan is no different from other developed countries. "The U.S. market, which is 30 percent larger than Japan's, has only five makers. Britain and France have only one each," he noted. Regarding keiretsu relationships, Furumoto explained that "Asahi Glass has 157 affiliated wholesalers in Japan, but we are not restricting the sale of other makers' products. Our executives have visited major wholesalers to explain that we are imposing no restrictions on sales."

Japan's Ministry of International Trade and Industry (MITI) had previously investigated U.S. complaints about trade barriers in the glass market but found no evidence of exclusionary agreements between domestic glassmakers and distribution and processing firms. To ensure openness, however, MITI asked the three firms to draw up guidelines to prevent exclusionary arrangements. The glass companies complied with this request in late 1991, but MITI regarded their initial guidelines as too abstract and urged the companies to set up programs that would be more practical and easier for employees to use, such as manuals showing concrete examples of violations of the Antimonopoly Law, and in-house workshops and committees to ensure compliance with the law.

Japan's Fair Trade Commission (JFTC) began its own investigation and concluded in June 1993 that the nation's three major plate glass manufacturers were obstructing free market competion by maintaining a monopoly and by forcing distributors to sell only their products. The commission investigated customary business practices in the automobile, auto parts, plate glass, and paper industries, and said they found no serious infringements of the Antimonopoly Law in the other three industries, although "some of them still give rebates and practice other dubious market-share building strategies." They did find, however, that in the market for plate glass it is customary for the three manufacturers to bind distributors with product supply contracts that prohibit them from selling other manufacturers' products. Such contracts obstruct other manufacturers, especially foreigners, from distributing their products, the JFTC said. Thier survey found that 399 flat-glass wholesale shops exist in Japan, 97 percent of which have long-term contractual relationships of more than five years with one of the glass producers. Of this group, 84 percent have maintained the same close ties for over 20 years. Only 12 of the wholesale shops dealt with more than one glass manufacturer. The JFTC decided that the glass companies were not in violation of the antitrust laws, but encouraged them to improve the market's "transparency."

MITI quickly jumped in with the FTC and ordered the three glass companies to "more thoroughly" abide by the Antimonopoly Law and to review their practice of paying rebates to middlemen. According to MITI, the glass makers' rebate system has encouraged wholesalers to concentrate on products of only one maker because the rebates increase as sales volumes increase, thereby discouraging purchases of small amounts of glass from other vendors. It has also been conventional practice to offer additional discounts to general contractors who encounter cost overruns after completing a construction project. The various rebates and discounts combine to create a situation in which the "real" price of glass may not be set until over a year after delivery. In response, Asahi Glass abolished its rebate system in January 1994, and the two other glass makers did so three months later.

The JFTC's findings sparked controversy throughout the construction materials industry, from flat glass and aluminum sash to cement, regarding the long-standing general constructors' practice of accepting contracts only from material manufacturers in their keiretsu, or business group. Often, non-keiretsu materials makers must offer their products at large discounts in order to win against firms affiliated with the general constructor. The system under which general constructors buy their materials was also criticized for the opportunities it creates for political corruption. However, "the problems surrounding the entire construction industry will not be resolved by constructions materials makers," said one industry association official, acknowledging that the materials suppliers do not have power to press the general constructors to change.

In March 1994, MITI released the results of another survey of glass wholesalers. Of the 342 respondents, 39, or 11.4 percent, said they handled foreign-made flat glass. And 58 more, or 17.0 percent, said they plan to handle foreign products in the near future. MITI interpreted these figures not as evidence of a closed market, but rather as signs of improvement. The ministry's survey found that among the sheet-glass wholesalers that currently do not sell foreign glass, 76 percent said they have not even been approached by foreign glass suppliers. Yasuhiko Furukawa, managing director of Asahi Glass, said the survey results prove that the domestic glass suppliers do not prevent wholesalers from handling foreign-made glass. "The fact that only a little over 10 percent of wholesalers deal with foreign glass suggests that the sales efforts by foreign glass makers, and the merits of handling foreign glass, are insufficient," he said.

MITI's interpretation of its survey results provides a good example of why foreigners are often suspicious of the ministry's pronouncements. An increase in the percentage of wholesalers handling foreign glass means little if they have handled only a token quantity. "For half the 39 wholesalers dealing with foreign glass, foreign products account for less than 1 percent of their total volume," points out Jun Okawa, executive director of Guardian Japan Ltd. "MITI conceals that fact, stressing only points that support its position," he adds. A MITI official acknowledged that most wholesalers are still "in a trial phase" of buying foreign glass. However, he said, American glass makers "should stop relying on the government to sell their products in Japan."

At least one U.S. glass company, PPG Industries Inc., would disagree with the characterization that they are relying on the government to sell their products. PPG is the largest manufacturer of glass in America. In July 1990, PPG and the Japanese trading conglomerate Itochu Corp. established a joint venture sales company in Japan, PPG-CI Co. The venture has faced an uphill battle. A company official said they could not even get an appointment with a wholesaler during their first two years. After nearly five years, volume had increased enough to allow PPG-CI to open a new ¥50 million sheet glass cutting center in Mie Prefecture to handle glass from PPG's U.S. and Chinese factories. They plan to open a second cutting center in the Tokyo area before 1996. Do they think the market is now open? Consider this: PPG-CI President Yoshisuke Mae will not disclose who he is leasing the premises for his cutting facilities from—for fear the lessor will suffer discrimination.

Sources: "Glass, Paper New Sources of Friction," *Daily Yomiuri*, December 17, 1991; "Glassmakers Adopt Anticartel Guidelines," *Japan Times*, December 17, 1991; "MITI Tells Glassmakers to Form Looser Market," *Japan Times*, January 25, 1992; "FTC Finds Glass Makers Block Fair Competition," *Daily Yomiuri*, June 30, 1993; "Fair Trade Panel to Glass Makers: Improve Transparency," *Japan Economic Journal*, July 5, 1993; "Construction Materials Industry Sees Chance to Change Business Practices," *Daily Yomiuri*, July 21, 1993; "No More Plate Glass Discounts," *Yomiuri Report from Japan*, January 6, 1994; "MITI: Foreign Sheet Glass Makers Not Competitive," *Yomiuri Report from Japan*, March 8, 1994; "Sheet-Glass Market Open to Foreign Firms, MITI Insists," *Nikkei Weekly*, March 13, 1994; "Major Sheet Glass Makers Abandon Kickback System," *Yomiuri Report from Japan*, March 30, 1994; and "Foreign-Affiliated Venture Cuts Into Flat-Glass Market," *Nikkei Weekly*, February 13, 1995.

In summary, concerns about trade barriers in Japan may receive inordinate political attention and may be given undue credibility because of Japan's large trade surplus with the United States. Yet regardless of the correlation between barriers and the trade gap, the concerns are genuine and do put considerable strain on what all parties agree is a vital economic relationship. To ignore, deny, or otherwise dismiss issues surrounding barriers because their relationship to bilateral trade flows may be inconsequential does not further constructive dialogue, timely resolution of the problems, and stronger ties between the United States and Japan.

A QUESTION OF IMPORTS

Despite the popular image in America of Japan as an aggressive exporting nation, researchers have largely reached a consensus that Japan's exports are not excessive (Lawrence 1987, Lincoln 1990). It is the volume of imports and Japan's openness to foreign products that are questioned. During the past decade, econometric analysis of actual trade flows has produced mixed results, supporting both the contention that Japan's imports, particularly of manufactured goods, are abnormally low (Balassa 1986, Balassa and Noland 1988, Lawrence 1987, 1991b, Lincoln 1990, Prestowitz, Chimerine, and Willen 1993), and, considering Japan's comparative advantages and scarcity of natural resources, that they are not (Bergsten and Cline 1985, Leamer 1988, Saxonhouse 1986, 1989, 1993). It is an undisputed fact that Japan imports an unusually small share of the manufactured goods it consumes when compared with other industrialized nations. The point of contention arises over explanations of why this is so. Some claim that when allowance is made for Japan's competitive strengths, lack of natural resources, and distance to trading partners, the level of manufactured imports is tenable. Others see an aberrant pattern of trade even after allowing for Japan's peculiar situation. While taking neither side of the argument, Srinivasan (1991) identifies two weaknesses of these studies:

> There is no basis in trade theory for the hypothesis that Japan's import penetration ratios ought to be comparable to those of other high-income industrialized countries. Furthermore, . . . none of the empirical studies and simulations *di-*

rectly links the observed import penetration ratios of Japan with appropriately defined and measured indicators of the extent of barriers to trade. Yet the fact that the simulations as well as the econometric studies, in spite of the differences in their methodology, sources, and extent of bias, all point in the same direction suggests that the issue will remain an open question (pp. 176–77).

PURPOSE AND SCOPE OF THIS RESEARCH

There has been considerable research regarding barriers inhibiting foreign direct investment in Japan, the policies and practices of the Japanese government and bureaucracy, and the exclusionary relationships typified by the large corporate groups known as the keiretsu. These studies and their findings are reviewed in Chapter 2. Another general area of alleged barriers consists of various types of anticompetitive behavior, which is frequently cited as an impediment against foreign manufacturers attempting to enter Japan.

This study will attempt to answer two critical questions relative to the occurrence of anticompetitive behavior in Japan: (1) Does anticompetitive behavior occur more frequently in Japan than in the United States? and, if so, (2) Does the occurrence of anticompetitive behavior in Japan have a negative impact on the performance of American companies marketing manufactured goods in Japan? This research goes beyond what has been done previously by investigating specific anticompetitive acts rather than inquiring about barriers in general. The results have implications for U.S. businesses attempting to enter or build their businesses in Japan, as well as U.S. and Japanese government policy makers, trade negotiators, and law enforcement officials.

The balance of Chapter 2 is devoted to the topic of anticompetitive behavior in Japan and its role, if any, in the repulsion of foreign manufactured goods. Evidence from the business community, price trends, and law enforcement practices are reviewed, and the antitrust laws of the United States and Japan are compared. Hypotheses are proposed regarding the relative occurrence of anticompetitive behavior and its impact on the performance of U.S. companies marketing manufactured goods in Japan. A model is then developed for use in testing the hypotheses.

The occurrence of specific anticompetitive behaviors in Japan has apparently not been studied earlier due to its sensitive and possibly illegal nature. Chapter 3 describes how a research instrument was developed to facilitate the collection of data without requiring the disclosure of potentially incriminating information. The Japan operations of almost 200 large U.S. multinational corporations were surveyed using the questionnaire, with considerable respondent interest and a high response rate. The variables used to operationalize the model are also explained in Chapter 3. Chapter 4 details the empirical test of the hypotheses using the data collected, and Chapter 5 summarizes the resulting conclusions and implications.

2

Entry Barriers and Antitrust Enforcement in Japan

Does Japan maintain a peculiar pattern of international trade? Do Japanese policies and practices intentionally block imports of manufactured goods? Do trade barriers in Japan restrict market access for foreigners? These questions have fueled vitriolic debate in political, academic, and commercial circles for more than twenty years. Conclusive resolution remains elusive. Both those who declare that Japan's trade is normal (considering its factor endowments and particular economic situation) and those who assert abnormality corroborate their position with empirical research, although methodological or theoretical flaws in the evidence are inevitably pointed out by proponents of the opposite view.

This chapter reviews the literature regarding Japan's pattern of trade, in particular the country's imports of manufactured goods and three broad and overlapping categories of alleged barriers: (1) government policy and practice, (2) exclusionary business relationships, and (3) anticompetitive practices. The bulk of this chapter focuses on the issues surrounding anticompetitive behavior. The antitrust laws of both the United States and Japan, including their historical development and enforcement, are briefly summarized. Hypotheses are developed regarding the occurrence of anticompetitive behavior and its impact on the performance of U.S. businesses marketing manufactured goods in Japan. The conceptual framework shown in Figure 2.1 and discussed below is used to help structure the research, identify variables for measurement, and test the hypotheses. The chapter closes with a brief review of the literature supporting the components of the model.

Figure 2.1
Conceptual Framework

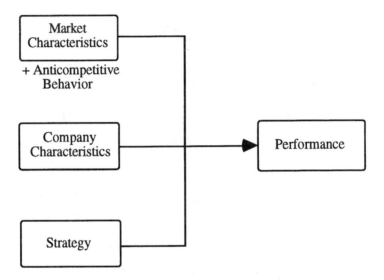

CONCEPTUAL FRAMEWORK

Madsen (1987) reviewed 17 empirical investigations of export performance and found over 350 different operationalized variables. He categorized these multiple variables into more general concepts that fit within a slightly modified version of Thorelli's (1977) Strategy + Structure = Performance paradigm. The model postulates that a firm's performance is a function of its environment, its organizational structure, and its strategies (Figure 2.1).

Various configurations of these factors (excepting anticompetitive behavior), their relationship to performance, and their interrelationships and feedback effects have been the subject of considerable study since the early work of Bain (1959). The relevant literature will be briefly reviewed later in this chapter. It is, however, the relationship between anticompetitive behavior and performance that will be the overriding concern and focus of this study. Prior research findings will be used to operationalize the model, into which measures of anticompetitive barriers will be introduced, enabling a determination of the significance of impact on business performance.

JAPAN'S IMPORTS

To build both a proper foundation for this research and an understanding of the circumstantial evidence behind foreign allegations of anticompetitive behavior, it will be useful to review prior studies investigating Japan's pattern of international trade, in particular the country's imports of manufactured goods. A summary of these studies is presented in Table 2.1.

Bergsten and Cline (1985) compared Japan with other developed countries on the basis of total imports as a percentage of GNP. They found that the Japanese import ratio does not differ significantly from other industrialized countries, and that most of Japan's trade imbalance with the United States can be explained by macroeconomic factors: the rapid U.S. recovery, the imbalance in both countries between savings and resources used for investment and fiscal deficits, and the overvalued dollar. They conclude that Japan's imports of manufactured goods do not suggest a higher level of protection than exists in the United States or Europe.

Saxonhouse (1986) used 1964, 1971, and 1979 data taken from 109 industries in 22 developed and developing countries (excluding Japan), and then attempted to predict Japan's trade structure using equations derived from the Heckscher-Ohlin factor endowment theory of trade structure (Heckscher and Ohlin 1991, Ohlin 1933). Instances where actual Japanese trade flows differed significantly from his forecast intervals accounted for only 6.1 percent of Japan's gross external trade, leading him to decide that "no special aberration of low imports that might be attributable to distinctively high, but intangible, Japanese protection needs to be conceded" (p. 247). Saxonhouse conducted further studies (1989, 1993) with some variations and more recent and expanded data, all reaching similar conclusions: that when full allowance is made for Japan's comparative advantages and distinctive national endowments, Japan's trade flows conform to international patterns.

Table 2.1
**Summary of Econometric Research Investigating Japan's
Pattern of International Trade**

Researchers	Findings
Japan's Pattern of Trade Is Normal	
Bergsten & Cline 1985	Japan's ratio of total imports as a percentage of GNP does not differ significantly from other industrialized nations.
Saxonhouse 1986	Instances of Japan's trade flows falling outside *ex post* forecasted intervals account for only 6% of Japan's gross external trade.
Saxonhouse 1989	Japan's trade flows conform to international patterns considering Japan's national resources and comparative advantages.
Srinivasan 1991	Questions the theoretical basis for the expectation that Japan's pattern of trade should be similar to other industrialized economies.
Saxonhouse 1993	Japan's unusual trade pattern can be explained by unusual factor endowments, without reference to industrial policy or anticompetitive barriers.
Japan's Pattern of Trade Is Abnormal	
Balassa 1986	Japan's total, primary, and manufactured imports are all significantly different from the import behavior of other developed nations.
Lawrence 1987	Japan's manufactured imports are 40% lower than expected for a typical industrial economy.
Balassa & Noland 1988	Japan's ratio of manufactured imports is extraordinarily low relative to the U.S., France, Germany, Italy, and the United Kingdom.
Lincoln 1990	Japan's imports of manufacture goods, as a percentage of both GDP and domestic output, are much lower than other developed nations. Japan's pattern of trade defies all expectations generated by intra-industry trade theory.
Prestowitz, et al. 1993	Compared with other developed countries, Japan's imports of capital goods and consumer products are unusually low. American exports to Japan are substantially lower than U.S. penetration of other OECD markets.

Balassa (1986) looked at trade patterns of total imports, primary imports, and manufactured imports for 18 developed economies. In all three cases, his results showed Japan to be an outlier "irrespective of whether one considers imports from all sources, from the industrial countries, or from developing countries" (p. 750), and even when allowing for the effect of changes in currency exchange rates.

Lawrence (1987) used the Helpman and Krugman (1985) model of international trade with 1970–1983 production and trade data from 22 industries to compare Japan's import behavior with twelve other industrialized countries. He discovered that Japan's imports of manufactured goods were significantly below those of other developed nations, and pointed out that because "manufactured goods account for less than a third of Japanese imports, even a substantial under-importing of manufactured goods is not likely to be detected in the aggregate specification" (p. 523). He attributed Japan's abnormally low level of manufactured imports to (1) a comparative advantage in producing manufactured goods, (2) the distance from its trading partners, and (3) trade barriers and an abnormal bias for Japanese-made products (the model could not differentiate between the effects of these two factors). He estimated that Japan's manufactured imports were about 40 percent lower than one would expect of a typical industrial economy.

Contrasting the ratio of manufacturing imports to domestic consumption for the United States, France, Germany, Italy, the United Kingdom, and Japan, and adjusting for differences in natural resources, population, per capita income, and distance to other markets, Balassa and Noland (1988) concluded that Japan's ratio of manufactured imports is extraordinarily low relative to the other countries examined.

Comparing Japan's imports of manufactured goods as a percentage of both GDP and domestic manufacturing output, with 17 developed and four developing nations over an 18–year period between 1970 and 1987, Lincoln (1990) found not only that Japan's figures are "startlingly lower" than any of the other countries, but that while most other economies expanded their imports of manufactured goods over time, there was relatively little or no change in Japan, a finding he believes is highly suggestive of protectionism. He concluded that "Japan does indeed exhibit an aversion to manufactured imports and avoids the two-way trade in many manufactured products that characterizes the international trade of other nations" (p. 2).

Lincoln also looked at intraindustry trade, which, as the term implies, is the international exchange of goods within the same industry. For example, the United States both exports and imports significant volumes of automobiles, office equipment, and machinery. Intraindustry trade may at first glance seem to contradict the theory of comparative advantage, but Lincoln shows how a relaxation of some unrealistic assumptions in the theory (e.g., perfect competition, absolutely identical products, an absence of economies of scale, and static efficiency) allows for the existence of intraindustry trade and a closer description of real-world economic activity. Research of intraindustry trade patterns has identified several general trends (Loertscher and Wolter 1980): (1) intraindustry trade increases as a nation's economy develops; (2) intraindustry trade is higher between countries with similar market sizes; (3) intraindustry trade rises when market barriers fall; and (4) different industries have characteristics that affect intraindustry trade regardless of national location. After analysis of data from 1970 to 1985 for France, Germany, Japan, South Korea, and the United States, and allowing for many of the hypotheses of why Japan might be different, Lincoln sums up his research by writing: Any way the question is posed, Japan turns out to be extraordinarily different. Its pattern of behavior is seriously at odds with all the expectations generated by intra-industry trade theory. . . . Its behavior has been distinctive in a way that is prejudicial to the economic interests of its trading partners, and in a way that does not characterize the interaction among other industrial nations" (p. 60).

The Economic Strategy Institute (Prestowitz, Chimerine, and Willen 1993) conducted an analysis of Japanese trading patterns using three separate models: (1) an econometric model for import shares across 23 countries, both in the aggregate and industry by industry; (2) an industry-by-industry, sector-by-sector analysis of Japanese imports; and (3) an industry-by-industry analysis of U.S. exports to Japan in comparison with U.S. exports to other countries. In every analysis, Japan's import behavior was anomalous. Imports of virtually all capital goods and consumer finished products were unusually low. American exports to Japan were substantially lower than U.S. penetration in other OECD (Organization for Economic Cooperation and Development) markets.

That Japan imports relatively fewer manufactured goods than other industrialized nations is now a largely uncontested, "well-established fact" (Lawrence and Schultze 1990, p. 35). The controversy surrounds explanations of why Japan's manufactured imports are so low, if the volume can be labeled abnormal, and if the relative absence of imports can be attributed to trade barriers. As noted above, some researchers ascribe Japan's peculiar pattern of trade to particular comparative advantages, a lack of natural resources, and the distance from its trading partners. Other studies that attempt to allow for these factors continue to find Japan to be an outlier.

Bergsten and Cline (1985) suggest that looking only at manufactured imports is unfair because resource-poor Japan must pay for its raw materials by maintaining a surplus in manufactured goods. Lawrence (1987) disputes this by comparing Germany and Japan, which he claims have similar natural resource endowments, and showing that low levels of manufactured imports are not necessarily required in resource-poor countries. And Lincoln (1990) maintains that "there is no persuasive economic argument why larger raw material imports should necessarily limit manufactured imports" (p. 20).

Saxonhouse has been perhaps the most prolific proponent of the point of view that ascribes normality to Japan's pattern of trade considering the country's specific economic conditions, and thus his work has attracted considerable attention. His model is faulted for comparing Japan against a sample that includes many developing nations that also have significant barriers to manufactured imports, thereby masking what might otherwise appear to be aberrant behavior were only industrialized countries considered (Balassa 1986, Lincoln 1990, Tyson 1989). The model relies on static assumptions that do not correspond with dynamic economic realities, such as assumptions that consumer tastes are homothetic, production technologies are identical across countries, and economies of scale are small (Tyson 1989). And his results are questioned because they fail to detect known cases of protectionism, such as finding nothing unusual with Japan's rice trade despite the fact that Japan had (until 1993) a complete ban on rice imports (Bergsten and Noland 1993).

Srinivasan (1991) reviews the work of some economists who attribute the discrepancy in manufactured good imports to the existence of barriers and some who do not. He finds methodological or theoretical weaknesses in all of the studies. For example, according to Srinivasan, Lawrence's (1987) equations are misspecified and suffer from a potential simultaneity bias, Saxonhouse's (1986) estimating equations may contain a simultaneity bias as well as heteroscedasticity in residual variances, and Balassa and Noland's (1988) model is not based on a reasonably well-specified theory. More importantly, Srinivasan questions the theoretical basis for the expectation that Japan's pattern of trade should be similar to other industrialized economies. He points out that "even if some of the estimation biases of these studies are ignored and their findings are accepted, it does not necessarily follow that . . . trade barriers are the *causal* factor explaining low Japanese imports" (p. 164). The same critique is raised by Saxonhouse (1989), faulting researchers who suggest that there is something distinctive about Japan's trade structure, while failing to make it clear why this distinctiveness should be associated with possible trade barriers.

There is also the opinion that the failure of U.S. businesses to penetrate Japan's markets more effectively has not been due to trade barriers, but is rather a result of the indifference of American companies, their misunderstanding and ignorance of Japan's markets and culture, a lack of determination and effort, the inferior quality of American-made products, and America's declining competitiveness (e.g., Alden 1985, Ishihara 1989, Jatusripitak, Fahey, and Kotler 1985, Lazer, Murata, and Kosaka 1985, Montgomery 1991, Terutomo 1986).

Abegglen and Stalk (1985) suggest that the strategies of many American (and other Western) firms entering the Japanese market were destined to fail. The typical company offered a new and technologically superior product at a high price, accompanied by the intensive service and education necessary to encourage diffusion into the marketplace. Within a short time, Japanese companies would take advantage of the consumer education and market development pioneered (and paid for) by the Western firm, offering a similar product with limited features and services but a lower price. The foreign firm would initially maintain the high end of the market, but eventually the faster growth and increasing volumes in the low-end market allowed the domestic Japanese firm to match and sometimes exceed the quality and technology of the Western product. At that point the Western firm had few options available in order to generate the volume and revenues to compete effectively. Had the priorities of Western businesses been more closely aligned with their Japanese competitors toward market share rather than profits, achieving "growth beyond the competitors' growth" (p. 59), the situation could look quite different today.

The same authors contend that all too often, strategic Japanese markets have been "yielded by too many Western competitors without a fight" (p. 214). The direct investments of foreign companies in Japan account for only 2 to 3 percent of total economic activity compared with between 10 and 20 percent in the United States and Europe. This variance in foreign investment has been due to two types of protection:

> The first type of protection was—but is no longer, and has not been for some years—from Japanese government regulations and restrictions on foreign investment. The second type of protection—no less effective and much more lasting—has been provided by the indifference and ignorance of possible foreign investors regarding Japan, and their unwillingness in many cases to pay the price in effort and patience to make the investment (p. 217).

With a contrary point of view, Encarnation (1992) argues that as Japan's formal government controls on foreign direct investment were liberalized, private restrictions continued to deny access to foreigners. A similar conclusion was reached by Mason (1992), who examined the pattern of foreign direct investment in Japan from 1899 to 1980 and found numerous instances where American and other foreign companies made "extraordinarily intensive efforts" to set up operations in Japan, but were denied entry through a combination of formal and informal investment restrictions "designed to promote the interests of indigenous industry" (p. 3). Mason acknowledges that some American companies did not make substantial efforts to invest in Japan, but explanations for this behavior become tautological, that is, if the lack of effort was due to indifference, was the indifference due to first-hand or observed failure of prior efforts?

> Numerous other American firms, including some of the nation's oldest, largest, most experienced, and most competitive multinationals, managed to achieve, at best, only limited in-

vestment "success" in Japan even after enormous commit-
ments of technology, managerial resources, and other assets.
The generally difficult experiences these multinationals encountered, together with the powerfully discouraging signals
such experiences communicated to other American firms who
might consider investing in Japan, significantly limited overall
levels of American investment. Rather than U.S. multinational
"neglect" of or "indifference" towards the Japanese market so
often emphasized in previous accounts, . . . the importance of
Japanese restrictions in impeding U.S. investment in modern
Japan therefore merits greater emphasis (p. 247).

Similar tautological concerns can be raised regarding the allegations that American businesses have not shown the tenacity, patience, and long-term vision necessary to develop the relationships
required to be successful in Japan. Lincoln (1990) points out that
it is an undisputed fact that Japan, with the consent and cooperation
of the U.S. government, was virtually closed to foreign businesses
during the first two decades following World War II. It was during
this period that the close business and social ties so valued by
Japanese culture either evolved or were reinforced exclusively
among Japanese companies. Thus, "the reasoning becomes circular: the relationships developed when foreigners were kept out, and
now their absence is taken to imply that they [foreigners] cannot
adequately understand or participate" (p. 90). Yamamura (1982)
questions whether the much-vaunted propensity of Japanese managers to take a long-term view toward business operations and
investments is a genuine attribute or simply a rational response in
a climate where MITI guidance, coordination, and protection
minimized exposure and risk. Tyson (1989) suggests that perhaps
Japanese consumers' alleged preference for Japanese goods may be
the result of closed markets that either encouraged or necessitated
such a preference. Are the "highly choosy preferences of Japanese
consumers" (Shimizu 1993) innate, or a result of decades during
which price was virtually eliminated as a differentiating variable
in a consumer's selection process due to formal or informal price
cartels, leading consumers to place greater emphasis on quality,
packaging, delivery, and other nonprice factors?

Charges of American indifference and ignorance beg the question of why Americans have been able to establish successful
operations in so many other international markets outside Japan.

Encarnation (1992) studied competition throughout the developed and developing countries of the world, finding that U.S. multinationals have created and sustained competitive advantages in nation after nation except in Japan. In addition, he noted that outside Japan, U.S. and Japanese multinationals pursue markedly similar strategies, and that Japanese companies operating in the United States have implemented "nearly every trade and investment strategy still denied in Japan to American multinationals—but successfully implemented by the Americans elsewhere in the world" (p. 8). In his review of intraindustry trade, Lincoln (1990) found that "Japan accepts few imports from the United States in precisely those areas of U.S. worldwide competitive strength" (p. 7).

On the other hand, Abegglen and Stalk (1985) point to many successful foreign companies in Japan and ask why others could not have done the same:

> Those companies that have a full appreciation of Japan's importance, and a conviction that they will do what is required to build a major position in Japan, have done so. Nestlé, IBM, and NCR took their prewar positions to major strengths in the postwar period; ITT, GE, and Siemens did not. The difference was not Japanese government regulations. Coca Cola and AMP took full advantage of the yen company route; most companies did not. The difference was not from Japanese obstacles. Texas Instruments drove its way into a major position in Japan; Motorola, Fairchild, RCA and Zenith did not. The Japanese government and Japanese discrimination do not account for the difference. Merck and BOC spent years working to the position they now have; others could have done so too (p. 239).

One thing is clear: neither those who attribute the relatively poor performance of U.S. business in Japan to American apathy, nor those who point to obstacles erected by the Japanese, will ever lack in evidence to support their position (See Episode 2.1 for a recent example from the trade battle between Fuji Photo Film and Kodak). It seems most accurate to conclude that both are correct. Many U.S. firms did dismiss Japan as a war-torn nation with little economic potential. Many companies did misjudge their marketing strategies and their Japanese competitors. And many savvy multinational firms have been unable to duplicate in Japan the success they have experienced elsewhere in the world, despite their considerable efforts. Thus acknowledging that no single factor bears full responsibility for the current state of U.S.–Japan commercial affairs, it is the primary objective of this study to further an understanding of what particular barriers to trade currently exist and the impact of those barriers on the flow of foreign manufactured goods into Japan.

<h3 style="text-align:center">Episode 2.1</h3>

A Heated Trade Battle—The Market for Photographic Film

A heated trade battle between the United States and Japan fired up in the summer of 1995 when, on May 18, Kodak filed a petition with the office of the U.S. Trade Representative (USTR) under Section 301 of the Trade Act of 1974. Within 45 days, as required by the law, USTR responded, announcing its intention to investigate Kodak's claims that U.S. photographic products are excluded from Japan's distribution system because major distributors and retail stores discourage their sale and because of the anticompetitive activity of Fuji Photo Film Co., whom Kodak accuses of group boycotts, price fixing, and cash payments to financially strapped wholesalers and retailers to facilitate control, maintain retail prices, and exclude outsiders. Kodak asserts that Fuji has instructed its agents not to sell products other than its own, and has ensured loyalty by paying rebates. Kodak's chairman George Fisher insists his company has lost $6 billion in revenues since 1975 through well-documented anticompetitive trade practices by Japan and Fuji Photo. Fuji refutes the charges.

Kodak and Fuji have been fighting for years, perhaps more frequently in the United States. In March 1994 the U.S. Commerce Department ruled against four Japanese photo film makers for dumping color photographic paper on the U.S. market. Commerce calculated the dumping rate at which the Japanese companies lowered prices for the U.S. market compared to identical products in Japan at between 321 and 360 percent, an unusually high rate. Kodak claimed that Fuji, which dominates the Japanese color printing paper market, and other makers set prices high in Japan and use the profit to cover the costs of dumping in the United States. In their defense, the Japanese companies noted Kodak's 70 percent share of the U.S. market in claiming that their actions had not harmed the U.S. industry.

There was a period when Fuji's dominance in Japan was challenged by domestic rival Konica, due to the increase of minilabs. The minilabs receive film from customers and process and print the film inside small outlets. Though this development shook Fuji for a time, Fuji soon included the minilabs in its network through controlling the supply of printing paper. As a result, Fuji's sales network was further strengthened.

To support its latest petition, Kodak compiled a huge, 250–page memorandum. Citing ministry reports, industry sources, and Japanese news media accounts, the memorandum argues that Fuji and Japan smothered Kodak's access to the Japanese photographic market by setting up exclusive agreements between Fuji and four distributors that handle nearly 70 percent of all photographic products in Japan. "The exclusive dealing arrangements placed on the distributors by Fuji have resulted in the distributors dropping competing products and being forced into a vassal position by Fuji," the memorandum contends. Kodak's CEO George Fisher claims that even though Kodak contacts the distributors in Japan, "there is a great sense of nervousness about going counter to what's in Fuji's best interests." Fisher explained that by filing its complaint with USTR, Kodak hopes to achieve better market access. "In a free and open world trading system, there is no room for partial participation in any major marketplace. (Kodak needs) access to the entire consumer market in Japan, rather than roughly 30 percent. If we appeared in as much of the Japanese market as Fuji appears in the U.S. market, we would be doing significantly better."

Kodak says the exclusionary practices did not exist until the 1970s, after Japan dismantled official trade restrictions, such as tariffs, and Kodak's film exports subsequently shot up. Alarmed, Japan and Fuji joined forces to create more subtle trade barriers, and Kodak's exports to Japan plunged. To support that allegation, Kodak cites a 1970 survey by the Japan Fair Trade Commission that found that "with respect to [consumer photographic] and X-ray films, most [distributors] are exclusive dealers. . . . It is believed that these changes are being made as the manufacturer's measures to counter trade and capital liberalization."

Both Fuji and the Ministry of International Trade and Industry (MITI) have rebuffed Kodak's arguments. Though Fuji does hold 70 percent of the Japanese film market, the numbers are reversed in the United States. According to industry figures, Kodak holds about 9 percent of the Japanese film market, compared with Fuji's 12 percent share in the United States. Furthermore, Fuji correctly points out that, while Japan has not placed import duties on color film or color paper since 1990, the United States imposes duties of 3.7 percent on similar imports from Japan. Concerning a kickback system for franchised stores, Fuji's Managing Director Masayuki Muneyuki says, "The kickback is made only when necessary, as in sales promotion. It is a business secret. But if Eastman Kodak makes public its kickback system, we will do the same."

Regarding Kodak's quest for market access, Muneyuki responds, "Kodak already has much access. There are 280,000 retail outlets in Japan, and 33,500 of them are photo shops and 14,500 are supermarkets and volume discount shops. These 48,000 constitute 17 percent of the number of outlets but they sell 73 percent of the volume of color film sold in Japan. Kodak has business with most of these outlets, apart from the question of how much business. The remainder are train station shops, dry cleaners, cigarette shops and other small outlets. But Kodak lumps them together and says it cannot get access to 70 percent of Japan's retail outlets. If it wants further access, it needs to invest more, building a network of photo-processing laboratories. If it competes better in marketing, it can get more access."

Many industry executives agree that the government used to collude with Fuji to keep Kodak out of the market, but they say that while Fuji may be benefiting from this now, the practice has ended. Kodak insists it persists. There is little doubt, however, that a big reason for Fuji's popularity is that for years it was virtually the only name in town. Moreover, it had significant help from the Japanese government during the industry's formative years. Tariffs on imported rolls of film hovered at 40 percent for years, and quotas restricted those imports. Then, before the government liberalized regulations on foreign investment in Japan, it issued guidelines in 1970 that were intended to prevent Kodak, which had a nominal presence in the market, from expanding and driving everyone else out. "We were afraid that Kodak would use its own capital strength to control the market with huge incentives like low prices, or attach some kind of gift to the films. Then, after ruling the market, they would raise the price," says Makoto Yokota, deputy director at the chemical products division at MITI. "There was this worry, so we issued guidelines so that the competition would be fair." The government sees the measures as promoting competition. But to many Americans, they are proof of collusion between the government and industry in Japan to restrict American products.

Kodak and American trade negotiators say that in the small stores across Japan, where more film is sold than through big retailers, Fuji uses its weight to bully storekeepers and distributors into only carrying its film. Kodak argues that it cannot convince Japan's four largest distributors to carry its products because Fuji effectively controls them, even though they are supposed to be independent. Fuji says its only stake in the companies is less than 20 percent ownership in two of them. "I know in the past, Fuji pressured their special wholesalers, but it happened 20 years ago," says Hiroshi Takahashi, president of Nihon Jumbo Co., which independently processes and sells 1.5 million rolls of film through 40,000 outlets in Japan. "They are Fuji film distributors, so naturally they sell Fuji film. Kodak's claim is like asking a Nissan dealer to sell a Toyota car."

In October 1995, Kodak filed data with USTR showing that the wholesale prices for photographic color film in Japan are 2.8 to 4.1 times higher than the prices of Japanese color roll film exported to major world markets. The data showed that the retail price of Fuji film in the United States is less than half the price of Fuji film sold in Japan. Kodak believes that the data bolsters its argument that the Japanese market for consumer photographic film and paper is closed. In response, Muneyuki blasted Kodak for citing only numbers that would support its allegations, and said the U.S. film giant had committed "grave methodological and calculational errors." He accused Kodak of intentionally magnifying the price gap by comparing prices in Japan on Fuji color film, which includes sales and distribution costs, with export prices, which do not include these costs. He also claimed that the prices Kodak quoted for Fuji film in the United States are for "secondary brand films," which are not sold in Japan.

As noted earlier, Fuji frequently points out that each company holds a similar share of the other's home market. But with prices so much higher in Japan, the profits each company earns in its domestic markets differ dramatically. Fuji obtains more than 90 percent of its operating profit from domestic sales, and enjoyed the fifth highest corporate earnings in Japan in 1994. "One of Kodak's main reasons for going after Fuji," suggests Jonathan Rosenzweig, an analyst at Salomon Brothers Inc., "is that they think if they take away Fuji's profit sanctuary in Japan they will get pricing pressure to ease elsewhere in the world." Kodak has not discounted its own brand name film in Japan, but has teamed up with four Japanese partners to sell private brand or co-branded film at up to half the regular price. The German film maker, Agfa, a unit of Bayer AG, has already swallowed a chunk of Fuji's business by selling private-brand discount film for as much as 60 percent less than Fuji film, increasing its market share from 1 to 4 percent.

Sources: "U.S. Rules Japanese Photo Film Makers Dumped Picture Paper," *Yomiuri Report from Japan*, March 31, 1994; "Kodak CEO Describes Exclusionary Tactics in Japan," Eastman Kodak Co. Press Release, May 31, 1995; Helene Cooper, "Kodak Has a Strong Case Against Japan, Analysts Say," *Asian Wall Street Journal*, June 12, 1995; "Kodak Questions Sales by Fuji Photo Affiliates," *Daily Yomiuri*, June 15, 1995; Masaichi Nosaka, "New Trade Battle Looming Over Photo Film Sales," *Daily Yomiuri*, July 2, 1995; "Fuji, Kodak Dispute Escalating into Potential Trade War," *Yomiuri Report from Japan*, July 4, 1995; "Fuji to Issue Official Rebuttal to Eastman Kodak Claim," *Yomiuri Report from Japan*, July 5, 1995; Sheryl WuDunn, "The Angle Determines the Picture: Fuji Says it Can't See What Kodak is Complaining About," *International Herald Tribune*, July 6, 1995; "Fuji-Kodak Battle Looms as Next Trade Dispute," *Yomiuri Report from Japan*, July 27, 1995; Malcolm Foster and Sandra Jones, "Inroads by Kodak, Agfa Put Fuji Shares Under Pressure," *Mainichi Daily News*, September 3, 1995; "Kodak Files Fuji Film Price Complaint with USTR," *Yomiuri Report from Japan*, October 19, 1995; "Fuji Refutes Kodak's Claim of Price Gap," *Yomiuri Report from Japan*, October 20, 1995; Tom Diederich, "Kodak Head: Fuji Fight Matter of Principle," *Daily Yomiuri*, October 21, 1995; "Fuji Photo to Kodak: Stand On Your Own," *Nikkei Weekly*, October 23, 1995; and Hisayuki Mitsusada, "The Picture Shows Unfair Access, says Kodak," *Nikkei Weekly*, October 23, 1995.

BARRIERS TO TRADE

Using 1983 data on trade flows and production, Harrigan (1993) computed "coverage ratios" for every type of nontariff barrier listed in a comprehensive inventory of nontariff barriers compiled by the United Nations Commission on Trade and Development. (The coverage ratio is a measure of the percentage of imports covered by one or more nontariff barrier.) He found that Japan had the highest overall weighted nontariff barrier coverage against imports of manufactured goods (40 percent) of the ten developed nations in his sample. Japan's level of nontariff barriers was substantially higher than the other countries.' The next highest overall ratio was for France, with 27 percent. Looking at bilateral comparisons, Harrigan computed Japan's coverage ratio against U.S. imports at

38 percent, more than double the 18 percent ratio he computed for U.S. barriers against imports from Japan.

Using a different subset of the 1983 United Nations data and a different methodology, Leamer (1991) concluded that 62 percent of U.S. exports to Japan faced some form of non-tariff barrier, while 35 percent of Japanese exports to the United States encountered similar barriers. He also noted that Japan's barriers disproportionately affected sectors of U.S. specialization. Harrigan's and Leamer's estimates vary considerably, but the proportion of Japanese barriers to U.S. barriers is consistent at approximately double. These findings add credibility to the claim that U.S. businesses face unusually high nontariff barriers in Japan, but controversy remains surrounding the impact of these barriers on actual trade flows: Harrigan concluded that the barriers are not associated with lower imports, while Leamer determined that barriers have a large import-reducing effect.

Various studies of exporting in general have identified factors such as high tariffs, import regulations, different product specifications and standards, and weak intellectual property laws as significant impediments faced by exporters (Bauerschmidt, Sullivan, and Gillespie 1985, Kedia and Chokar 1986, Rabino 1980, Thomas 1989). Ryans (1988) looked specifically at exports to Japan and analyzed the impact of multiple variables on Canadian exporters. He surveyed a sample of business people in Canada who were knowledgeable about the history of their company's products in Japan, and found that market share was lower for those products where nontariff barriers were believed to have slowed penetration. (Ryans used only the term *non-tariff barriers* without further description.)

The American Chamber of Commerce in Japan (ACCJ) has provided a detailed description of the types of barriers businesses believe they currently confront in Japan, identifying "several recurrent issues which represent major obstacles to fair access to the Japanese market" (p. 3) in its 1993 Trade White Paper (American Chamber of Commerce in Japan 1993). The ACCJ catalogues 14 recurrent issues, but these can be grouped into three broad and overlapping categories: (1) matters of government policy and practice, (2) keiretsu organizations and exclusionary business relationships, and (3) anticompetitive practices. The first two categories will be briefly reviewed before taking an in-depth look at the third.

Government Policy and Practice

The ACCJ decries "actions on the part of the Japanese government and industry to preserve advantages for domestic companies through regulations and practices designed to prevent 'disruptive competition' and protect the status quo" (ACCJ 1993, p. 5). Many of the barriers detailed by the ACCJ are matters of government policy and bureaucratic practice: (1) incompatibility of many Japanese standards, certification procedures, and testing practices with internationally recognized criteria, and reluctance to accept internationally approved measures as applicable in Japan; (2) excessive regulation; (3) lack of transparency in formation, dissemination, and enforcement of rules and regulations; (4) inadequate protection of intellectual property rights; (5) unnecessary obfuscation created by problems of classification or definition of terms; (6) tariffs and quotas; and (7) government procurement practices. In a survey of academic researchers, business practitioners, and government officials from America, Europe, and Japan, government trade barriers and bureaucratic practices were reported to be "moderately important" impediments for foreign companies in Japan (Czinkota and Kotabe 1993). See Episodes 2.2 and 2.3 for two illustrative examples.

Episode 2.2
Bureaucratic Red Tape or Trade Barriers?—The Case
of Amorphous Metals

Amorphous metals were developed by Allied Signal, Inc. during the early 1970s. They are created by rapidly cooling alloys of iron, boron, and silicon, giving them a glass-like consistency with exceptional electrical and magnetic properties. One of the most immediate and popular uses of amorphous metals was to replace the silicon steel cores in electric transformers. When electric current passes through a transformer, electricity is lost as waste heat. Amorphous metal cores reduce this loss by 70 percent, having a substantial impact on a nation's energy consumption. It was estimated that the United States would save over 100 million barrels of oil annually if existing silicon steel transformers were replaced with amorphous metal transformers. In addition, amorphous metal transformers are safer to operate and require less frequent maintenance. As a result, by the end of the 1980s, over 30,000 transformers with amorphous metal cores had been installed in the

United States, accumulating years of combined operating experience, all without a single failure.

Because the cost of electricity in Japan is nearly double that of the United States, and considering Japan's dependence on energy imports and the Japanese government's active efforts to encourage energy conservation throughout the country, it was expected that amorphous metals would find a good market there. With over 7 million commercial transformers in use in Japan, a switch to amorphous metal would save 30 million barrels of oil annually and the need to build two new electric power plants. In fact, the Japan Research & Development Corporation (JRDC), a government organization, awarded substantial funds to several Japanese companies to incorporate amorphous metal technology into their products. So in 1981, Allied Signal established a joint venture with the Mitsui Group called Nippon Amorphous Metals Company Ltd. (NAMCO) to market the product in Japan, and then entered into discussions with Nippon Steel for a license as the primary supplier. Nippon Steel was able to duplicate the technology, but would not commit to a licensing agreement. JRDC told Allied plainly that if the technology and basic patents were not licensed to all JRDC members, those companies would find a way to evade Allied's patents.

Allied applied for a Japanese composition patent in 1973. It was granted eleven years later, in 1984. Allied applied for a process patent in 1977. It was issued twelve years later, in 1989. Yet Japan's patent law required that the basic product and process technologies behind Allied's amorphous metals be publicly disclosed within 18 months of filing. And because patent life in Japan runs for 20 years from the date of filing, Allied's patent protection would begin to expire in 1993.

There are nine public utilities in Japan. Tokyo Electric Power Company, or TEPCO, is the largest. When Allied's Japanese affiliate NAMCO first marketed the new technology, the public utilities stated that amorphous metals were thermally unstable. In response to this argument, NAMCO provided data regarding thermal stability available from General Electric. The Japanese utilities refused to accept the data, saying is was unacceptable because it was not collected in Japan. But within a short time, TEPCO's own research showed that amorphous metal core transformers are thermally stable and maintain their energy efficient features throughout their lifetime.

With this argument gone, the utilities then complained that the price of amorphous metal was too high. This seemed dubious considering

Japan's own studies, which indicated that amorphous metal transformers would save the country $1 billion worth of electricity annually. But in response, NAMCO reduced the price to 1.5 times that of silicon steel, a level that transformer manufacturers and TEPCO had stated would make the product economically competitive.

The utilities then claimed that transformers using amorphous metals are too bulky and would mar the beauty of Japan's streets. The reality is that these transformers are only 10 percent larger than those using silicon steel, a difference that is hardly noticeable on top of a utility pole.

By 1990, all of the Japanese transformer manufacturers had developed the ability to manufacture amorphous metal transformers. TEPCO had tested amorphous metal transformers for more than four years, with excellent results. But no utility had begun installing them, and none had any plans to do so. It appeared to Allied that the utilities were boycotting amorphous metal until Allied's patents expired and Japanese companies could supply the materials. Allied was the exclusive holder of both the Japanese product and process patents, and operated the only commercial amorphous metal production facility in the world. Allied had invested 12 years and millions of dollars attempting to open a market in Japan for a product with proven superior economic and societal advantages, all to no avail, due to what appeared to be deliberate roadblocks and delay tactics. Allied had expected sales of $100 million annually, but after 12 years had yet to achieve more than a tiny fraction of that amount. So on March 5, 1990, Allied filed a petition with the U.S. Trade Representative's office accusing Japan of unfair trade practices.

In April 1990, USTR began talks with Ministry of International Trade and Industry officials over the amorphous metal market. USTR reviewed Allied's efforts to enter the Japanese market and the roadblocks encountered. MITI responded that the reliability and cost-efficiency of amorphous metal had yet to be established. It contended that purchasing by private companies was a matter of choice in which the government should not interfere. MITI claimed that the amorphous metals consortium funded by JRDC's ¥1.6 billion subsidy was merely a study group in which foreign firms would have been welcome to participate. MITI also rejected the notion that JRDC had interfered with licensing negotiations because it was not an established fact.

By September 21, with America threatening retaliation, a settlement was reached. Japan agreed to buy enough amorphous metal for 32,000 transformers (0.5% of the market) by the end of 1993. The utilities would shorten their testing time from three years to one. And although the government refused to extend Allied's patents, Japanese steelmakers agreed to honor Allied's manufacturing patents until 1997 and not produce or sell the material without a license.

Sources: Allied Signal, Inc., "Presentation Before the United States International Trade Commission," January 26, 1990; "Negotiators Fail to Forge Pact for Amorphous Metal Trade," *Japan Times*, May 15, 1990; "Amorphous Metals Talks Seen Collapsing," *Mainichi Daily News*, September 5, 1990; Tsuyoshi Sunohara, "Tokyo, Washington Near Accord on Amorphous Metals Dispute," *Japan Economic Journal*, September 8, 1990; "Low Tricks in High Tech," *Economist*, September 29, 1990.

Episode 2.3
Bureaucratic Red Tape or Trade Barriers?—The Case of CNN

While Allied bombs were dropping all around Peter Arnett in Baghdad during the Gulf War, television viewers from Riyadh to Reno eagerly tuned into Cable News Network (CNN) to hear his live reports. In Japan, they mostly got the story second hand. When the war broke out, thousands of inquiries poured in from Japanese viewers seeking to plug into CNN programs, according to Takashi Kobayashi, executive vice-president of Japan Cable Television Ltd., a supplier in Tokyo of the Atlanta, Georgia–based cable station.

But the Ministry of Posts and Telecommunications, which controls and allocates radio waves in Japan, prohibits individual viewers from subscribing to CNN or to any other program transmitted to earth through communications satellites. CNN is available in Japan only through cable TV, which is available only in isolated pockets of Japan. CNN is viewed by some 400,000 people in Japan, compared with 54 million households in the United States and about 9 million in Europe. Indeed, Japanese viewers are virtually the only ones among the world's leading economies who do not have free access to CNN.

Many analysts say the major reason the telecommunications ministry prohibits communications satellite operators from directly servicing individual customers is that the entry of foreign program suppliers would pose a threat to domestic broadcasters. Still another possible explanation is that NHK, the Japansee government-controlled broadcasting system, is anxious to start up its own global network, and would like to get a grip on the home market before CNN makes a serious challenge. In any event, the sudden surge in interest in the American network has brought Japan's protected broadcasting market into the limelight and given rise to criticism that the telecommunications ministry is not serving the interests of consumers.

Analysts say the ministry especially wants to protect Japan Satellite Broadcasting Inc. (JSB), a joint venture of 193 big Japanese firms that in April 1991 started commercial service using a broadcasting satellite. The government sees the JSB venture as part of its policy to promote the development of the satellite business in Japan, they say.

"We understand that more competition is inevitable in the future," said Toshiyuki Shinohara, a director of the National Association of Commercial Broadcasters in Japan. "But a slow, phased deregulation is necessary, during which all parties, including the new entrants, should equally bear some burden." A telecommunications ministry official added that excessive competition in the communications market does not serve consumers' interest. "A balanced orderly transition," he said, "is a must."

As one concession to those clamoring for change, the telecommunications ministry amended the Broadcasting Law in October 1989, opening the way for "some" communications service providers to operate as broadcasters using communications satellites. But the ministry has yet to come up with the selection criteria for such companies. In the meantime, JSB and NHK may have acquired more subscribers, and the new service providers will face a hard time finding new customers.

Source: Adapted from Yuko Inoue, "CNN Blockage in Japan Stirring Criticism," *Japan Economic Journal*, May 11, 1991.

Some of the same complaints have been echoed by Japan's most powerful business lobby. Keidanren backed a bill submitted to Japan's Diet that will significantly reduce the power of government ministries to influence business decisions through the use of "administrative guidance." The bill gives a company receiving administrative guidance a legal right to demand documentation from the ministry explaining the purpose and substance of the guidance, and the name of the government official responsible. It also requires the ministries to act on applications in a timely manner or to justify, in writing, any delays. This will limit the ministries' ability to cajole compliance with their administrative guidance by sitting on applications and withholding necessary government approvals (*Nikkei Weekly* 1991). For quite some time, Keidanren has also strongly advocated the deregulation of particular industries and practices (Keidanren 1990b and 1991; see also Uekusa 1990 for a summary of the regulatory environment in Japan). Isao Nakauchi, the chairman of Daiei, Japan's largest supermarket chain and a member of the Administrative Reform Promotion Council's Import Promotion and Market Access Improvement Group, recently complained that government bureaucrats are sabotaging his panel's efforts to increase imports and improve market access (*Yomiuri Report from Japan* 1994). He complained that instead of cooperating, the bureaucrats only explain "why easing of restrictions is impossible." One of the most powerful "revolutions" unfolding in Japan in the 1990s is the rise of renegade retailers who are either finding ways to circumvent regulations, or simply ignoring them, with popular support from consumers. Episodes 2.4 and 2.5 are examples of this new trend.

Episode 2.4
Renegade Retailers—Airline Tickets

Sakae Travel Service Co., a Nagoya-based travel agency, created a stir in late 1993 when it began selling drastically discounted airline tickets on domestic travel. Discount air tickets have been common on international routes, but very rare on domestic travel. Commercial airlines and the Transport Ministry were reportedly irked by the development, charging that discount tickets introduce disorder to the air travel market and irritate those who have purchased tickets at regular prices. Transport Ministry Vice-Minister Michihiko Matsuo said he did not welcome the new bargain tickets and would launch an investigation. There is nothing illegal, however, about the marketing of discount airline tickets. Airlines are required by law to sell airline tickets at predetermined prices, but travel agents are not.

While the Transport Ministry may be unhappy, consumers clearly welcome the cheaper tickets. Sakae Travel has received more than 600 inquiries a day about the bargain tickets since it began accepting advance bookings in mid-September, 1993. Half of the inquiries have resulted in actual purchases. Airlines and flight numbers cannot be chosen. A person makes an advance purchase by designating only the route and the day of travel. Prices differ according to the day of the week, but still manage to be 30 to 50 percent lower than regular fares. A Tokyo-Sapporo ticket, for example, sells for ¥21,500 ($199), compared with the regular price of ¥43,100 ($400).

Source: Adapted from "Government Officials Irked by Air Ticket Discounts," *Yomiuri Report from Japan*, November 4, 1993.

Episode 2.5
Renegade Retailers—Gasoline

It is a business practitioner's dream—setting prices artificially high and keeping them there even when costs go down, without any worries about competition. For years, this has been reality for those running Japan's petroleum industry. At around ¥120 per liter on average, gasoline prices are several times higher in Japan than in the United States, and refiners make handsome profits on sales. Companies cooperate with each other in setting prices, with the blessing of the Ministry of International Trade and Industry and the Fair Trade Commission. Bureaucrats have their hands on the crude oil tap, divvying up quotas to refiners.

The petrochemical industry first formed a marketing cartel in 1983 to sell polyethylene, polypropylene, and other plastic products. In the midst of a recession, they were desperately trying to pare their enormous deficits. MITI approved the cartel as a stop-gap measure on the grounds that many firms risked bankruptcy otherwise. Seventeen petrochemical companies set up four joint sales firms. Business bounced back soon after the cartel was formed and demand picked up. Several years later the industry was posting record profits, but the cartel was still setting prices. The "stop-gap" measure has become a permanent feature of the industry, making petrochemical companies a lot richer and angering clients who are sharply critical of the institutionalization of the cartel.

Banding together in times of trouble is a common trait of the Japanese business community. Defenders of the system say it is not that Japanese business people are adverse to competition, but there is a certain feeling that it is better to live and let live. Japanese business leaders do not like to see someone breaking ranks to get a jump on the others—and they are willing to call on government ministries to hammer down the nails that stick out. As a result, they often play into the hands of government bureaucrats interested in "guiding" an industry in a certain direction.

MITI has treated the oil industry more as a utility than as a competitive business. In exchange for accepting slim margins on heavy oil and naphtha for industry, Japanese oil companies have been allowed to charge motorists high gasoline prices. The average price of gasoline at the pump in Japan is ¥126 ($1.05) per liter, almost four times the price in the United States. But after decades of compelling the country's crowd of tiny oil companies to operate as a cartel, MITI has now decided it wants just the opposite: more competition and consolidation. MITI hopes that, out of the ensuing scramble, a Japanese oil giant capable of competing against the world's biggest and strongest firms will emerge. Japan has 26 oil companies that do all their own refining, and none of them ranks among the world's top 50 oil companies. The largest, Nippon Oil, is only a fifth the size of Exxon or Royal Dutch/Shell. In 1986 MITI announced a five-year plan to inject competition into the industry. But it was not until March 1992 that it abolished its refining quotas, the biggest obstacle to open competition.

As is frequently the case, however, the leading catalyst for change comes from renegade retailers who create an awareness among consumers that prices and practices can be different. In the gasoline industry, public dissatisfaction with the government's complex and rigid system for licensing gas station operators intensified following the opening of an unlicensed filling station in Nagoya that began selling gasoline at cut-rate prices. For one liter of gasoline, the new unlicensed station charged ¥100, which is ¥15–20 cheaper than the rates at regular filling stations licensed by MITI. The station, opened by Kanare Beikoku, a rice retailer in Komaki, Aichi Prefecture, attracted so many customers that police were called in to control traffic as cars formed long lines in front of the establishment.

Complicated paperwork based on the Gasoline Sales Law must be filled out before MITI issues a license granting permission to operate a gasoline station. Kanare filed itsr paperwork in December 1993, but left a portion blank that asks about the source from which gasoline will be procured. MITI refused to issue a business license because Kanare did not disclose its gasoline procurement routes, which MITI claims is a must in order to "supply quality gasoline on a stable basis." A lawyer representing Kanare says his client refuses to divulge its source because to do so would only compromise the firm's interests and prevent it from offering cheaper gas prices. "The Gasoline Sales

Law only stipulates in a few lines that each gas station should identify its procurement routes. But MITI has been expanding its interpretation of this clause in order to interfere with market competition using what it calls 'administrative guidance.' Under the present circumstances, we do not see any obligation to follow MITI," he declared. Kanare subsequently decided to open the station anyway on May 18, 1994, without a business license.

MITI has not taken any legal action against Kanare, which continues to operate its gas station without a proper license. MITI was expected to settle the dispute through dialogue, instead of legal action. But on May 30, 1994, an organization representing 25 gas station operators filed a lawsuit with the Nagoya District Court against Kanare. Takeo Yamaguchi, who serves as the group's director, emphasized that the purpose of the suit is not to shut down Kanare's gas station, but to change the present law that rigidly controls the distribution of gasoline. Yamaguchi stressed that his organization and Kanare are fighting for the same cause—to change MITI's control over gasoline distribution—but that only their strategies differ. What prompted the organization to take its legal action against Kanare, he said, is the deep-rooted distrust of MITI among gas station operators. What Kanare and Yamaguchi's organization want is the freedom to procure gasoline and sell it at whatever price they choose.

Sources: "Japan's Petrochemical Cartel: Idea Whose Time Has Passed?" *Japan Economic Journal*, May 12, 1991; "Japan's Oil Industry: Ready, Set, Compete," *Economist*, October 10, 1992; "Renegade Gas Station Fuels Debate over Government Regulation," *Yomiuri Report from Japan*, June 3, 1994.

Much has been written about the role Japan's government has played, and continues to play, in the country's economic development (e.g., Eads and Yamamura 1987, Frost 1987, Itoh, Kiyono, Okuno-Fujiwara, and Suzumura 1991, Jatusripitak, Fahey, and Kotler 1985, Johnson 1982, Komiya, Okuno, and Suzumura 1988, Kotabe 1984, Krugman 1987b, Lincoln 1984, Matsushita 1987, Noland 1991, 1993, Okuno-Fujiwara 1991, Pempel 1987, Prestowitz 1988b, Rapp 1986, Schultz 1987, Sekiguchi and Horiuchi 1985, Uekusa 1987, van Wolferen 1989, Yamamura 1967, 1982, 1990). Many of these writings are of a theme consistent with the Organization for Economic Cooperation and Development's findings from their 1972 study of Japan's industrial policies (OECD 1972): "It is clear that Japan's outstanding economic performance since the war is attributable largely to the close, purposeful co-op-eration between government, industry, the financial institutions and labor. Under MITI's guidance the nation's productive re-sources have been effectively marshaled towards the achievement of national objectives" (p. 170).

Staiger, Deardorff, and Stern's (1988) empirical study led them to conclude that there is some basis for the allegation that Japan embraces a commercial policy that substantially distorts its pattern of international trade. But there are many who disagree. It is undeniable that the government, led by MITI, adopted aggressive industrial growth policies, but the effectiveness and value of the government's involvement is questioned. "To suppose that politi-cians and officials in league with businessmen were able to plan and guide Japan's explosive economic growth in detail is neither credible in the abstract nor . . . supported by the realities" (Trezise and Suzuki 1976, p. 757). After reviewing Japan's trade patterns and industrial policies, Saxonhouse (1983) concludes that "if Japa-nese experience is properly normalized . . . there is little left to be explained by an industrial policy which is more than a substitute for market process" (p. 271).

Japan's semiconductor industry is a good example of the diverse interpretations of Japan's industrial policies and their impact. Anchordoguy (1989) thoroughly documents how Japan's state and corporate institutions and policies combined to promote the devel-opment and then the protection of the domestic computer and semiconductor industries:

> Major state and corporate institutions involved in Japan's national effort to nurture these industries frequently over-stepped the bounds of "fair play." Japan clearly did not have a comparative advantage in these areas when it decided to target them in the late 1950s. Initial policies may have been justified as support for infant industries. Yet government promotion and protection continued long after Japanese firms were estab-lished in the industry (Anchordoguy 1990 pp. 303-4).

Krugman (1987b) looks at the same industry in Japan and con-cludes,

The effects of industrial targeting in semiconductors are enveloped in fog. We do not know clearly the extent to which the industry was really targeted; we do not know how important the targeting was in international competition; and . . . it is unclear whether the government intervention which has taken place was either crucial for the industry or beneficial from a national point of view (pp. 293–94).

It is important to make a clear distinction between Japan's industrial policies that support particular industries that bureaucrats predict to become "winners" in global markets, and government policies and practices that protect the domestic market. While the two may be related, they are not necessarily one and the same. The failure of industries "picked" by MITI, and the success of others in spite of MITI, are well known and frequently cited as proof of the fallacies of industrial policy. But as Drucker (1994) explains, "though MITI neither anticipated nor much encouraged Japan's world market successes, the whole Japanese system is geared to running with them" (p. 107). Governments have an obligation to promote the economic well-being of their country. Many of Japan's practices that support domestic businesses (e.g., control of inflation, high investment in education and training, a tax system that encourages savings and investment) are sound policies found in other economically successful countries, and are areas in which the United States needs improvement, as was agreed in the Structural Impediments Initiative (SII) talks. Yet among the many aspects of Japan's probusiness climate described by Drucker, he also notes that the country "deliberately keeps prices and profits high in a protected domestic market in order to generate cash for overseas investment and market penetration" (p. 107). It is this perception that Japan has stepped beyond promotion and support to protection, and from cooperation to collusion, to which U.S. businesses object.

Entry theory postulates that incumbent firms can make investments that will deter entry and enlarge future profits (Caves and Porter 1977). Investments in excess capacity, research and development, proliferation of brands, exclusive distribution, vertical integration, and greater economies of scale can all create effective barriers to entry. These investments protect both the investor and his incumbent rivals as well. Individual outlays that vary from the point of profit maximization for the group of incumbents as a whole usually lead to conflict among the group and retaliatory actions that reduce efficiencies and profits for everyone. Caves and Porter explain how the effectiveness of these barriers can be enhanced through industry collusion:

> The entry barriers surrounding an industry can be viewed as a collective good, generating joint profits for the going firms. The individual firm's investment in this collective good therefore depends on a comparison of the outlay to the present value of the amount of increased joint profits that he expects to capture. Without collusion, incumbents will neglect the rents that accrue to their rivals and therefore invest less in entry barriers than the amount that maximizes joint monopoly profits. Hence an attractive form of collusion is a joint understanding on investment in entry barriers that internalizes these private external benefits and sets investment in entry barriers at the scale that equates the group's marginal revenue to each investor's marginal cost (p. 247).

It is clear that MITI, in particular, directed the necessary collusion among the incumbents of many industries in Japan to coordinate investment in the excess capacity, research, and development, exclusive distribution, vertical integration, and greater economies of scale that characterize Japan's development in the decades following the war. It is also very clear that MITI's and the government's involvement in Japan's industrial development has declined considerably during the past decade. But it must also be recognized that 20 to 30 years of world-class competitive international experience, coupled with a protected domestic market, could allow a country's industries to develop significant competitive advantages that would lead to long-term consequences well beyond the period of formal collusion and control (Tyson 1989).

Keiretsu and Exclusionary Relationships

Japan's large corporate groups, known as the keiretsu, are frequently cited as impediments to more open trade with Japan (ACCJ 1993, Cutts 1992, Holstein 1990, Johnson 1990a). Americans are initially suspicious of the keiretsu groups simply because they are linked together by means that are illegal in the United States: a combination of bank holdings (banks may hold up to 5 percent of the outstanding stock of a company), intercorporate sharehold-ings, and interlocking directorates (Flath 1993, Kotabe 1989). For example, in fiscal year 1989, the average ratio of intragroup stock-holding relations for the six largest keiretsu was 55 percent, and in 65 percent of the constituent companies the largest shareholder was another member of the same corporate group. In addition, the keiretsu are often accused of dealing predominantly with group members only and thereby effectively denying market access to foreigners. Foreign companies complain that due to the keiretsu or other business and government relationships, a strong "buy Japa-nese" bias keeps out foreign products even when quality and price are competitive or superior to the domestic alternative (ACCJ 1993, Czinkota and Kotabe 1993). For one example, see Episode 2.6.

Episode 2.6
Exclusionary Relationships?—Keiretsu in Japan's Paper Industry

The market for paper in Japan has been a source of trade friction with the United States throughout the 1990s. A settlement appeared to be reached in 1992, when Japan's paper distributors set a goal of pushing the market share of imports into double digits from less than 4 percent. Yet in October 1995, with the market share of imports unchanged and the U.S. share dropping from 1.8 percent in 1992 and 1993 to 1.7 percent in 1994, U.S. Trade Representative Mickey Kantor singled out the Japanese paper market as particularly closed.

Japanese paper company executives and government officials claim that the small market share held by U.S. companies is due to a lack of effort by American exporters. They question how serious U.S. paper manufacturers are about building a greater presence in the Japanese market, noting that many U.S. companies seem interested in Japan only when their own market is in a slump. For example, U.S. exports of corrugated cardboard to Japan were 149,000 metric tons in 1988, when the yen's average exchange rate was ¥144 to a dollar. In 1994 the volume dropped to nearly half, 76,000 tons, despite a much stronger dollar. "No wonder the question is asked here about how seriously U.S. firms really want to export," says Eiichi Katayama, an analyst at Nomura Research Institute. (In response to this particular claim, however, Americans point out that it is Japan's market for printing and writing paper that is suspected of market barriers, a much higher-value-added market than that for corrugated packaging paper.)

Japanese officials also claim that U.S. paper makers are not competitive in important segments of the Japanese market. For example, while U.S. producers are relatively competitive in high-end paper products made from virgin pulp, they rarely supply high-end products made of recycled paper, for which there is strong demand in Japan. The quality and suitability of U.S.-made paper is also questioned. "In the United States, good quality is judged to be that which is found to be easy to use in printing operations. So operations-efficient paper is high-quality paper," explains Jiro Kawage, chairman of New Oji Paper Co. and chairman of the Japan Paper Association. "In Japan, however, paper users are also engaged in stiff competition, so desirable paper is that which looks good to the eye and is easy to read. So high quality in the U.S. is not necessarily high quality in Japan."

U.S. officials point to two particular barriers in Japan's paper industry. The first is the practice of deferred price-setting, or *atogime*. Essentially, atogime is a hedging tool used widely in the paper and petrochemical industries that allows sellers to renegotiate prices after delivery. Although it leaves plenty of room for exclusionary price manipulation, defenders of atogime say it helps small firms stay afloat in times of price uncertainty. Deferred pricing became common in the paper industry in 1977, when the sector was still in the grip of the recession triggered by the 1973 oil crisis. But like many practices, atogime outlived the original event that gave rise to it. Although Japan's paper makers say the practice still affords them much needed flexibility, they abandoned retrospective price determination in 1994.

The American Paper Institute (API) also points to vertical keiretsu in Japan's market for printing and writing paper as an impediment to entry by U.S. paper companies. API commissioned a study that found "the printing/writing paper industry in Japan is characterized by strong vertical integration which often includes paper producers, distributors and end users within the same keiretsu." Japan's major paper producers hold significant equity shares in the major Japanese distributors and have close ties to printers and other end users. Some distributors have obtained credit from their paper suppliers, the study found. In addition, there appear to be close equity and lending relationships between banks and paper suppliers and distributors. "Empirical evidence demonstrates that a distributor will often source paper from suppliers with whom it shares a principal bank," claimed the API.

Japan's largest paper distributor, Japan Pulp & Paper Company, Ltd. (JPP), has over 1,000 suppliers, but three very large ones: New Oji,

Nippon Paper Industries, and Honshu. These three paper manufacturers supply 64 percent of the products sold by JPP. They also happen to be the four largest stockholders, with a combined ownership of 35 percent. The president of at least one of these companies sits on the board of directors of JPP. This situation is not unusual. In fact, all paper agents in Japan are partially owned by either Japanese paper manufacturers or Japanese trading companies. The agents have strong, but not exclusive, ties with the paper makers. Because no paper company produces all types of paper, the agents handle products from multiple manufacturers. Paper agents handle over 80 percent of the paper makers' output.

Sources: "Deferred Pricing Another Practice that Outlives its Initial Usefulness," *Nihon Keizai Shimbun*, April 28, 1990; "U.S. Claims Barriers Hurting Paper Sales," *Japan Times*, January 24, 1991; "Keiretsu in Japan's Paper Industry," *Regulation, Economics and Law*, October 17, 1991; "Glass, Paper New Sources of Friction," *Daily Yomiuri*, December 17, 1991; Kenichi Amano, "Paper Merchants in Bind Over U.S. Pact," *Nikkei Weekly*, May 23, 1993; Douglas Ostrom, "Japan's Paper Industry: Writing a New Chapter?" JEI Report No. 11A, Japan Economic Institute, March 26, 1993; "Japan, U.S. Clash over Paper Trade Issue," *Yomiuri Report from Japan*, September 21, 1995; "Japan Paper Market May Go on U.S. Watch List," *Yomiuri Report from Japan*, September 28, 1995; and Satoshi Isaka, "U.S. Rekindles Paper Dispute; Japan Cries Foul," *Nikkei Weekly*, October 2, 1995.

To test the validity of this charge, Kreinin (1988) studied the procurement practices of foreign-owned subsidiaries in Australia when purchasing capital equipment and machinery. He conducted interviews at 62 firms: 22 American, 20 Japanese and 20 European subsidiaries across multiple industries. He found that Japanese subsidiaries are controlled by local Japanese management and the parent company to a much greater degree than American or European subsidiaries, resulting in significantly less autonomy in purchasing and sourcing decisions. In the American and European subsidiaries, the origin of the existing machinery was spread evenly across sources in America, Europe, and Japan, but in the Japanese subsidiaries there was an overwhelming preponderance of Japanese equipment. When making new purchases, the American and European subsidiaries used international bids. Three-fourths of the Japanese subsidiaries did not use international bids and "most said that they never even considered doing so. In most cases they go directly to Japan and buy Japanese equipment. . . . To the extent that bidding is used it is confined to Japanese suppliers" (p. 537). As to the issue of quality, Kreinin found that there was no greater dissatisfaction with non-Japanese than with Japanese machines. He concluded that industrial structure and buyers' preferences are a barrier to the importation of manufactured goods in Japan.

In order to empirically test for an explicit link between the keiretsu and Japan's volume of imports, Lawrence (1991a) examined the impact of the keiretsu on exports and imports using a model designed by Petri (1989) to explain, across Japanese industries, the share of imports in domestic consumption and the share of exports in world markets. Lawrence used 1985 data for 37 industries and found that "there is a relationship between Japanese industries with unusually low imports by OECD standards and those in which vertical keiretsu predominate" (p. 329). In another study, Fung (1991) found that the keiretsu operations do contribute to an increase in Japan's trade surplus with the United States and other countries. Noland (1992) devised a model to correct for weaknesses in the work of Lawrence, Petri, and Fung, yet his results remained consistent with their findings: keiretsu organizations are associated with lower than expected imports.

Lawrence (1991b) also examined intrafirm trade flows between the United States, Europe, and Japan. In U.S. and European exports to each other, and in Japanese exports to the United States, the exporting country's firms dominate intrafirm sales. But intrafirm shipments from Japanese subsidiaries abroad dominate Japanese imports. Three-fourths of Japan's imports are handled by the nine largest general trading companies, the *sogo shosha* (Morimoto 1994). While one may ask what difference it makes if the trading companies take title in a Japanese or foreign port, the point is that the sogo shosha have considerable control over what gets into Japan. The key issue, then, states Lawrence, "is their willingness to import products that compete directly with domestic firms with who they have close relationships" (p. 22). He cites Gerlach's findings (1989) to suggest that they do not. In a later study of preferential trading patterns among the keiretsu, Gerlach (1992) writes, "various studies have demonstrated that actual empirical patterns across a range of relationships cannot simply be explained away as minor deviations from otherwise anonymous market transactions" (p. 84).

Saxonhouse (1991) dismisses Kreinin's findings regarding the purchase behavior of foreign subsidiaries of Japanese companies stating that such practices are "entirely consistent with the traditional histories of multinational corporations and overseas direct investment and do not suggest truly distinctive Japanese practices" (p. 42). He bases this conclusion on the proposition that the Japanese subsidiaries are of recent origin and maintain a comparative advantage, while the U.S. and European subsidiaries were established many years earlier and have lost much of their comparative advantage. Graham and Krugman (1989) propose a similar explanation for the higher than average import propensity associated with Japanese investments in the United States. They point out that the bulk of Japanese investment in the United States has occurred within the past 10 years and is, therefore, newer and less mature than foreign investors as a whole. "Numerous studies of the behavior of multinational firms indicate that as these firms become more experienced in the conduct of international operations they tend to increase the local content of the output of their overseas subsidiaries" (p. 60). Among these "numerous studies" is the work of Davidson (1980), who has shown that, regardless of nationality, newly established foreign subsidiaries tend to rely more on their parent companies for components and equipment. As time goes by and they establish reliable ties with local suppliers, imports from the motherland taper off. U.S. and European firms have followed similar patterns of overseas investment and development, only much earlier than the recent Japanese expansion abroad.

The Fair Trade Commission of Japan determined that the ratio of intragroup transactions as a percentage of total transactions within each corporate group was only 7.3 percent of sales and 8.1 percent of purchases, on average for the six largest keiretsu. These JFTC numbers are often cited as proof that the keiretsu do not engage in exclusionary practices (Imai 1990, Ministry of Foreign Affairs 1992), although deficiencies in the JFTC's method of calculation have been noted (Okumura 1990). In particular, the JFTC's figures account for intragroup trade between only the horizontal keiretsu members (e.g., 24 companies for the Mitsui group, 29 for Mitsubishi, 20 for Sumitomo). Yet each of these companies are connected with literally thousands of smaller firms in a vertical keiretsu (Yamamura 1990). When the combined transactions of the horizontal and vertical keiretsu are considered, "over one-half of Japanese interfirm trade involves closely affiliated keiretsu partners" (Gerlach 1989, p. 165).

Actual business transaction volumes among a horizontal and vertical keiretsu are presented in the appendix to this chapter for illustrative purposes. For confidentiality, the sales dollars are disguised although the percentage figures remain actual.

Without bickering over what exactly constitutes a keiretsu relationship, or how many exist, the larger issue at hand concerns the legitimacy of referring to these long-term relationships between Japanese manufacturers and their suppliers as trade barriers. Irwin (1994) suggests that the in-house production of parts by large American conglomerates is an equally exclusive commercial strategy. And, in fact, keiretsu arrangements offer some attractive benefits that are missing in a vertically integrated firm or with contractual relationships.

> The [keiretsu] supplier is an independent business subject to market disciplines rather than another bit of a big bureaucracy. From the supplier's point of view, the relationship is better than simply one based on contracts, price and open bidding. Though the supplier has no guarantee of the business, the firm can be fairly sure it will keep it for a long time. It can thus invest on the assumption that the contract will not last for merely a year (*Economist* 1991a, pp. 36–37).

Keidanren (1991) has defended the practice of exclusive business dealing as a rational economic response that emphasizes stable, long-term relationships based on trust. Keidanren also addressed the allegation that cross-shareholding contributes to exclusive trading within the keiretsu: "The truth is that business transactions are determined by purely economic considerations, such as price, quality, and delivery times. Cross-shareholding is a long-established practice and is used to foster stable management. It does not cause economically unreasonable transactions" (p. 26).

Kotabe's (1992) work in global sourcing adds considerable economic validity to keiretsu-like relationships. He has found that, irrespective of nationality, companies that procure key components in-house tend to enjoy higher market performance. "In-house" for Japanese firms includes procurement from within their vertical keiretsu group. Rather than attacking the keiretsu, foreign firms might be better served by attempting to imitate or join similar arrangements. However, due to the rapid appreciation of the yen and the prolonged recession in Japan, keiretsu relationships have also begun to show some schism among member companies. The dynamic of keiretsu relationships is illustrated in Episodes 2.7 and 2.8.

Episode 2.7
A Schism in Keiretsu Relationships—Japan's Steel and Automobile Industries

Japan's steelmakers and automakers alike were tremendously shocked when they learned that Mitsubishi Motors Corp. was testing the quality of cold-rolled steel sheets produced in South Korea. Cold-rolled steel sheets are used in motor vehicle doors. Japan has never used such South Korean products.

Japanese automakers are the biggest consumers of domestically produced steel. Steel sheets produced in South Korea cost about 20 percent less than domestic products. Because of the difference in quality, however, and because of long-established business relations, it was taken for granted that Japanese automakers would purchase steel sheets from domestic producers.

Mitsubishi Motors Corp. began a move that ran counter to the established business practice because the company has to be cost conscious. One person in the motor vehicle industry said, "In addition to the prolonged recession, a price war between Japanese and U.S. automakers has begun to hurt the Japanese motor vehicle industry. In the past rise of the yen, U.S. automakers followed Japanese automakers in marking up their products. Recently, however, they have launched a low-price offensive toward Japan. Japanese automakers have to be cost conscious."

Japan's steel industry, however, was also facing difficulties. Japan's five integrated iron and steel companies reported deficits totaling nearly ¥300 billion for the year ended March 31, 1994. Toshio Kogure, executive vice-president of Kawasaki Steel Corp., said that his company could not afford to lower prices at all. Kogure said he had been shocked when he was told by an automaker that it was possible to produce vehicles by using 50 to 60 percent imported steel, if not 100 percent.

The behind-the-scenes price negotiations between automakers and steelmakers in 1994 were unusually bitter, and that each side criticized the other's managerial inefficiency. One steel official said his company had made capital investment at an automaker's request, but demand for steel had declined as a result of the recession. Auto company demands for price markdowns were also unjustified, he said, because of the transfer of car production overseas.

The officer in charge of material purchases at an automaker retorted that his company had even cut manpower, that the prices of Japan-made steel products were high by international comparison, and that steelmakers were wrong if they thought they could continue business in a carefree manner.

Source: Adapted from "Some Cracks in Japan's Manufacturing Unity," *Yomiuri Report from Japan*, May 25, 1994.

Episode 2.8
A Schism in Keiretsu Relationships—Japan's Consumer Electronics

In 1992, Japan's Fair Trade Commission began investigating whether four of the country's leading electronics companies have been illegally propping up domestic prices of televisions, portable video cameras, and other popular home electronics products. The probe, which targets the sales affiliates of Matsushita Electric Industrial Co., Sony Corp., Toshiba Corp., and Hitachi Ltd., touches on one of the U.S. electronics industry's long-standing complaints against Japan's high-technology sector: that by keeping prices high in their domestic market, Japanese companies have been able to boost profits while selling products below cost abroad.

While symbolically significant, the case is limited in its scope and possible impact. The JFTC began investigating the sales arms of the four companies on suspicion of restricting the posted prices of certain electronics products. While some stores may negotiate lower prices with customers, the stores apparently have been restricted from advertising prices below certain levels. The JFTC is investigating the sales companies individually and not whether they acted as a cartel. If confirmed, the companies' pricing practices would constitute unfair trade practices, as described in the antimonopoly guidelines issued by the JFTC in July 1991. Unlike cases involving cartels, however, a finding of unfair trade practices would not result in financial penalties for the companies. Instead, the JFTC would issue an administrative cease-and-desist order to the companies, then monitor their compliance.

In a story repeated across multiple industries in Japan through the late 1980s and into the 1990s, the greatest change is resulting not from JFTC or other government action, but from retailers who buck the system. In the electronics industry, one such company is Step, a Tokyo area electronics retailer that sells for prices generally 30 to 40 percent lower than manufacturer's suggested retail and 10 to 15 percent below other discount stores. "Most Japanese discounters eventually give in to pressure from manufacturers, but we haven't," says Yoshio Terada, Step's 37–year-old founder. Terada is still a rarity in Japan's cartelized distribution system. Even in Akihabara, Tokyo's famous consumer electronics district, stores usually conform with retail prices set by the manufacturers.

Terada used to operate inside the system. He founded Step in 1977 as one of Matsushita Electric's network of around 18,000 "mom and pop" National stores. Matsushita gave Terada special rebates in return for his loyalty. But one day when business was slow, he cut prices on batteries by 20 percent. Executives of Matsushita's sales affiliate were dispatched to try to convince Terada to get back in line. He rebelled, and in 1983 the affiliate cut him off.

Terada, by now convinced that he was on to something with his price strategy, looked elsewhere. He began buying on the "gray market" from wholesalers. At first, manufacturers tried to force him out of business by trying to trace his suppliers. Sometimes Terada gets supplies by importing directly. For example, in the late 1980s he exploited the price gap between Apple computers in Japan and in the United States by importing Apples from the United States and under-cutting Apple's main distributor in Japan by 50 percent, until eventually Apple cut prices on its own.

Step now has seven outlets. In terms of annual sales per employee, a Japanese trade publication reports that Step, at $1 million per employee, is achieving nearly double the average for Japan's electronics retailing industry. Step's annual sales of nearly $30,000 per square foot are more than 25 times the industry average.

Sources: Christopher J. Chipello and Jacob M. Schlesinger, "Japanese Electronics Firms Face Probe of Pricing in Home Market," *Asian Wall Street Journal*, March 27, 1992; and Gale Eisenstodt, "In Step," *Forbes*, October 26, 1992.

Anticompetitive Practices

The balance of the trade barriers detailed by the ACCJ (1993) can be summarized as anticompetitive practices, and center around the contention that Japan does not sufficiently enforce its Antimonopoly Law (AML). The ACCJ claims that "flagrant violations" of the law go uninvestigated. U.S. trade negotiators echoed this accusation during the Structural Impediments Initiative talks and in the annual SII reviews: "The Government of Japan has not yet strengthened sufficiently its antimonopoly enforcement regime so that it will effectively deter collusive anticompetitive practices that exclude foreign competition in the Japanese market" (*First Annual Report* 1991, p. 7).

It is understandable how American executives living and working in Japan could get the impression that antitrust infractions are rampant. Reports of apparent violations of the AML (e.g., bid-rigging, price fixing, market allocation, refusals to deal, abuse of dominant bargaining position, restrictions on resale price, restrictions on dealings, etc.) appear frequently in Tokyo's newspapers, usually noting that either no or very light punitive action was taken. The six cases in Episode 2.9 are a few examples.

Episode 2.9
Japanese Practices That Lead Foreigners to be Skeptical

Paint

In December 1992, the Fair Trade Commission advised an association of Japan's 16 leading paint manufacturers to end an alleged price cartel that was in violation of the Antimonopoly Law. The association members, including Dainippon Ink and Chemicals Inc. and Nippon Paint Co., control more than 90 percent of the ¥15 billion market in Japan for surface paint used for marking such things as pedestrian crossings and centerlines. The JFTC said the manufacturers raised the price of their marking paint by ¥ 8 per kilogram in October 1991 according to their cartel agreement, and they prohibited member firms from competing for customers thereafter.

The cartel had made plans to raise the price by more than ¥ 5 from the following April, but the plan was uncovered when the JFTC made an on-the-spot inspection of an association member who was under investigation on suspicion of prearranged bidding for road marking ordered by local police agencies.

Water Meters

The Fair Trade Commission ordered manufacturers to stop fixing prices in the ¥40 billion market for water meters. Three major companies and some smaller firms in Tokyo, Osaka, and other areas are suspected of the practice. The three large companies, Kimmon Mfg. Co., Aichi Tokei Denki Co., and OKK Corp., are all listed on the first section of the Tokyo Stock Exchange. Over the past several years they have repeatedly fixed prices and negotiated among themselves to determine which companies should receive orders from local water bureaus.

Ink

Asahi Shimbun, citing industry sources, reported that officials from more than ten ink makers decided at a meeting in a Tokyo hotel in late August 1990 to coordinate price increases for their products. By early 1991, the ink makers had implemented about 40 percent of the proposed price increases after negotiations with customers. The makers cited a rise in pigment prices resulting from the Persian Gulf crisis and higher resin and solvent prices. Japan's Fair Trade Commission confirmed that it is investigating the printing-ink manufacturers for possibly conspiring to raise prices. A spokesman for Dainippon Ink & Chemicals Inc., one of Japan's biggest ink makers, confirmed that the company's offices were searched by commission officials in March 1991, but he added that the company has not been notified of the investigation's findings.

Electrical Equipment

The Fair Trade Commission officially filed a complaint in March 1995 against nine leading heavy electric machinery makers for allegedly rigging bids on equipment ordered by the Japan Sewage Works Agency. The JFTC alleges the firms violated Article 3 of the Antimonopoly Law, which bans unfair trade practices. The nine firms include some of Japan's best known companies—Hitachi Ltd., Toshiba Corp., Mitsubishi Electric Corp., and Fuji Electric Corp.

According to the JFTC investigation, the officials of the nine companies met on June 15, 1993, at Fuji Electric's headquarters to collude on a bid for installment of electric equipment in a sewage disposal plant commissioned by the agency. Seventy-five percent of the total contract was to be allocated to the five major companies and 25 percent was to go to the four smaller firms. The companies had begun meeting in 1990, and formed a coordination group that chose one company each year to serve as secretary. In 1993, Fuji Electric was the secretary.

The JFTC also found that officials of the Japan Sewage Works Agency were deeply involved in the bid-rigging case by setting up the range of the contract price for each company and letting the secretary company know budgets for each project. They also allegedly hinted the contract price to the secretary company.

The JFTC also revealed that the nine heavy electric machinery makers regularly divided up other orders for nuclear power plants, electric equipment at waterworks, and other facilities. Bid-rigging practices were only part of the complex system established by these firms to divide orders among themselves.

Later in the year the Tokyo High Public Prosecutors office indicted a former executive of the Japan Sewage Works Agency, the nine heavy machinery makers, and 17 of their employees for bid-rigging on public sewage projects.

Banking

For many years, Japanese banks were given free rein collectively to determine industry terms in accordance with Ministry of Finance directives, on everything from lending rates to corporate bond under-writing fees. For example, six of Japan's biggest banks (Dai-Ichi, Kangyo, Sumitomo, Fuji, Sanwa, Mitsubishi, and Mitsui) held regular "informal" meetings of their managing directors, at which Finance Ministry officials took part, to discuss important issues affecting the industry, including the setting of deposit rates.

During the Structural Impediments Initiative talks between the United States and Japan, the United States complained that Japan's Fair Trade Commission had neglected to enforce the country's antitrust laws within the banking industry, leading to higher costs for borrowers and a competitive disadvantage for foreign banks. In September 1992, upon his appointment as the new chairman of the Japan's JFTC, Masami Kogayu warned the banking industry that it would be the object of heightened oversight.

Mistubishi Bank drew up guidelines to ensure compliance with the antitrust laws and began a related employee education program. Among Mitsubishi's suggestions were that bank officials avoid exchanging information on interest-rate changes, deciding through interbank discussions which institutions will act as price leaders, and requiring clients to set up accounts to receive loans. Other banks, including Sumitomo and Sakura, prepared similar training materials for their employees. The Regional Banks Association of Japan issued an illustrated book to explain the antitrust law to bank employees. It outlines 12 examples of illegal practices, including cases involving industry gatherings as well as the collusive setting of lending rates and financial product sales.

Despite these highly publicized efforts of the banks, cases still abound of identical bank rates and lock-step changes. City banks continue to offer exactly the same short-term prime lending rates despite different funding costs. In response to criticism of these continued practices, the banks counter that "it is natural for lending rates to converge because free competition constricts differences." In April 1995, the Bank of Tokyo reduced the fee it charges for converting yen into foreign currencies by an average of 20 percent. For example, the rate for converting yen to the dollar was reduced from ¥2 to ¥1.8 per dollar. The Bank of Tokyo said the decision was aimed at improving services to customers, but considering that this was the first time the fee had been reduced in over 25 years, skeptics believed the action to have been prompted by the Japan's Fair Trade Commission's ongoing investigation of the adoption of identical commission rates by most banks.

Securities

Japan's Nikkei index of the Tokyo Stock Exchange is a measure of equity values similar to the Dow Jones index. The Nikkei climbed from 6,669 at the beginning of 1980 to a peak of 38,916 near the end of 1989, averaging gains of nearly 20 percent annually throughout the decade. Although it seemed that stock (and land) prices could only go up, what later became known as the "bubble economy" came crashing down, with the Nikkei shedding two-thirds of its value in a matter of months. This was a devastating loss for many, but a loss in which not all investors shared equally.

In the summer of 1991 it was revealed amid great scandal that Japan's major securities companies had, between October 1987 and March 1990, compensated certain major clients ¥128 billion ($950 million) for investment losses. That July the Ministry of Finance submitted to Japan's House of Representatives a detailed list of 176 private and public corporations and three individuals who received most of this compensation (¥105 billion) from Japan's "Big Four" brokerages: Nomura Securities, Daiwa Securities, Nikko Securities, and Yamaichi Securities. The securities houses used a variety of complex schemes to reimburse these select clients for stock market losses, but the most common method was through repurchases of equity warrant bonds and Japanese government bonds at up to seven times their value. The Ministry of Finance, which had been aware of the practice for at least several months, if not longer, had issued a directive in 1989 banning such loss compensation.

Two months later, in September 1991, the Ministry of Finance announced they had uncovered an additional ¥43.5 billion in loss compensation paid out between April 1990 and March 1991. In addition, the ministry acknowledged that selected clients were reimbursed not only for losses on the stock market but for profits that fell short of expectations. Nobuhiko Matsuno, the director-general of the Finance Ministry's Securities Bureau, reported to the House of Representatives on September 26 that between October 1988 and March 1991 a total of ¥9.97 billion in payments were made under "yield guarantee" agreements that were illegal according to Article 50 of the Securities and Exchange Law.

At the height of the bubble in 1988, and still after the crash in 1992, individual investors accounted for 40 percent of the shares purchased and sold on the Tokyo Stock Exchange. Considering that the average commission is higher for small individual investors compared with large institutions, Japan's consumers paid dearly and lost much more relative to their total financial resources, yet they received no loss compensation or yield guarantees. And although the loss reimbursements were in clear violation of Japan's securities laws and Ministry of Finance directives, the punishment for this illegal behavior was only that the Big Four were barred from underwriting government bonds for one month.

The official explanations of the payouts were somewhat incredible. The President of Nikko Securities, Kichiro Takao, told reporters that the decision to compensate clients for investment losses were made by division chiefs, and that top company officials were not aware of these illegal practices. To one familiar with Japanese business practices, the idea that division chiefs could authorize the payment of over ¥23 billion to 38 clients (as in Nikko's case) without the senior executives' awareness seems unbelievable. Despite the official listing provided by the Ministry of Finance, companies reported to have received the loss compensation denied the allegations when contacted by the *Yomiuri Shimbun*, Japan's largest newspaper. The single largest recipient, the Pension Welfare Service Corp., a public corporation under the Health and Welfare Ministry, was reportedly paid ¥4.9 billion ($36 million) from Nomura, yet told the *Yomiuri*, "It is inconceivable that we received such compensation." An official of Nagase Co., reimbursed ¥676 million by Daiwa, said "This is the first I've heard of any such payments or that we could have received them." "We have no knowledge of having received compensation," said a spokesman for Kawasaki Steel, reported to have received ¥801 million from Yamaichi.

Sources: "Paint Makers Advised to End Price Cartel," *Mainichi Daily News*, December 3, 1992; "Water-Meter Firms Fixed Prices," *Japan Times*, December 7, 1992; Christopher J. Chipello, "Tokyo Is Investigating Allegations of Collusion Among Ink Makers," *Asian Wall Street Journal*, March 3, 1992; "JFTC Targets Nine Companies for Bid-Rigging," *Daily Yomiuri*, March 7, 1995; "Banking Practices," *Far East Economic Review*, October 26, 1989; Hijiri Inose, "Bankers Feel the Heat of Fair-Trade Law," *Nikkei Weekly*, October 26, 1992; "Bank of Tokyo to Cut Fee for Converting Yen into Foreign Currencies," *Yomiuri Report from Japan*, April 14, 1995; "List of Compensated Firms Goes to Diet Committee," *Mainichi Daily News*, July 31, 1991; C. Tait Ratcliffe, "Loss Compensation, Individual Investors," *Mainichi Daily News*, August 8, 1991; "Big Four Paid ¥43.5 Billion to Clients After March 1990," *Japan Times*, September 25, 1991; and "Securities Firms Guaranteed Yields," *Yomiuri Report from Japan*, September 30, 1991.

The statements of Japanese government and business leaders may be even more influential in shaping the opinions of foreigners regarding the occurrence of anticompetitive behavior in Japan. Naohiro Amaya, a former vice-minister of foreign affairs, declared that "MITI has never adhered to the idea of a free economy in a traditional sense. From the start, its role was doomed to conflict with the principles of free trade" (*Nikkei Weekly* 1992). A former commissioner of Japan's Fair Trade Commission, Hiroshi Iyori, explained, "Government agencies have often intervened in the decision-making processes of businesses they administer. Some companies even complained they were engaged in bid-rigging because a government agency told them to do so" (*Nikkei Weekly* 1993). A top JFTC official involved in the SII talks, Yoji Sugiyama, was quoted as saying, "There is a chance that almost all regular business practices conducted in Japan may conflict with antitrust laws" (Fujigane and Ennis 1990, p. 28). Gaishi Hiraiwa, chairman of Keidanren, stressed at his organization's 54th annual general meeting in May 1992 that "Japanese companies need to practice free and fair competition under internationally accepted rules and to shift their emphasis from protecting producers to serving consumers' interests" (*Japan Times* 1992).

Japan's three largest construction companies, Kajima, Shimizu, and Taisei, submitted a 33–page document to the JFTC requesting that bid-rigging and collusive price fixing (known as *dango*) be allowed to continue within the construction industry because it is beneficial to the economy. Among the benefits cited were that dango (1) helps prevent companies from dumping and cutting corners, (2) protects small contractors from the threat of bankruptcy, and (3) prevents companies from winning contracts at too high prices, since a successful price is decided before bidding (*Daily Yomiuri* 1994b). The claim that bid-rigging serves the public interest is not new. The construction industry, backed by Keidanren, put forward the same argument in 1982 when the JFTC attempted to limit the occurrence of dango (Sanekata 1986). Kajima also issued a manual for company personnel encouraging better compliance with the AML. It contains the frank admission, "Unfortunately, our own firm has not been a model of obedience to the Antimonopoly Law" (*Mainichi Daily News* 1993b).

Eight companies indicted for fixing prices of plastic food wrap admitted their illegal behavior, but claimed the indictment was invalid because it is widely known that other industries in Japan also fix prices, and they were simply singled out as a scapegoat due to U.S. pressure for stronger antitrust enforcement (*Daily Yomiuri* 1992b). The court case is described in Episode 2.10.

Episode 2.10
Antitrust Enforcement in Japan: The Plastic Wrap Case

Eight manufacturers of the plastic food wrapping material commonly used in supermarkets have the dubious distinction of being the first companies since the mid 1970s to be indicted by the public prosecutor on criminal charges of violating the Antimonopoly Law. The eight companies, Mitsui Toatsu Chemicals, Mitsubishi Plastics Industries, Shin-Etsu Polymer, Denki Kagaku Kogyo, Nippon Carbine

Industries, Riken Vinyl Industry, Hitachi-Borden Chemical Products, and Gunze, together account for 98 percent of Japan's output of cellophane wrapping material.

The alleged cartel was formed at the senior executive level, and the decision was made to implement two stages of price hikes. During the first stage the corporations colluded to raise the price of their standard product, a three-kilogram package of 500 meters of plastic wrap, from ¥1,000 to ¥1,150 as of September 1, 1991. In order to make the price increase go smoothly, the corporations collectively decided to freeze their shares on the Tokyo Stock Exchange. In addition to this, a decision was made to keep extra orders of their standard product down to 30 percent just before they raised the price, so that the major users such as supermarkets and other large retailers could not buy as much stock at the cheaper price. The second stage of the price hikes involved a rise in price of the standard product by ¥250 from November 1. The group was allegedly using a customer complaints service as a front to ensure each of the eight corporations stuck to the price-fixing deal.

The Japaness Fair Trade Commission raided the offices of the eight companies and their trade association in April 1991. Soon thereafter, the eight firms informed the JFTC that they had agreed to dissolve the alleged cartel, virtually admitting that they had formed one. Katsuji Hoshi, general affairs manager for Mitsui Toatsu, expressed "deep regret" over the affair and admitted that his company had participated in negotiations with other makers to raise the price of wrapping material.

Commenting on the case, JFTC Chairman Setsuo Umezawa said, "The recent indictment may change the minds of the Japanese people about the Antimonopoly Law. We will continue to take action against any commercial acts which are found to be illegal." His remarks seemed to be prompted by recent criticism of the JFTC as "a house dog trained not to bite people," as one critic put it. Some Japanese officials have said that the JFTC's former weakness worked to the advantage of Japan's rapid economic development. It enabled Japanese firms to take concerted action in the process of expansion and to form cartels to distribute profits among themselves. Now that Japan has greater international responsibilities, however, it can no longer afford a meek commission or lax enforcement of the Antimonopoly Law. One JFTC official says, "Since Japan is now an economic superpower, foreign countries are not going to allow the nation's old commercial rules to prevail."

During the hearings at the Tokyo High Court in May 1993, lawyers representing the eight companies called the charges unjust and demanded that the indictment be dropped. While they admitted that the broad substance of the charges was true, they argued that the JFTC's complaints were a result of pressure stemming from the development of the Japan-U.S. Structural Impediments Initiatives talks, in which the closed nature of Japanese companies was the target of strong U.S. criticism. Citing the commission's failure to charge cement manufacturers in a similar but much broader operation, the attorneys argued that the wrap manufacturers were being made a scapegoat to alleviate U.S. pressure. The defense claimed that food-wrap manufacturing is a relatively small business, with annual sales of about ¥30 billion, so that pricing coordination did not significantly affect people's lives and therefore did not actually constitute a crime. They also maintained that it was necessary to form a price cartel to help clear deficits resulting from fierce competition practiced earlier within the industry.

The court was not convinced, finding the eight companies guilty of price fixing, and assessing each company fines of ¥6–8 million. Fifteen executives of the companies were given suspended prison sentences of six months to one year.

The case was widely regarded as an attempt to show that Japan's historically weak Fair Trade Commission was getting tougher. But if anything, the case came to symbolize the timidity of the commission. Critics said the agency was focusing on a minor case while not prosecuting much more serious cases, such as a huge construction industry bid-rigging case in a suburb of Tokyo. Indeed, that was the main plea of the defendants: that it was unfair to single them out since there were so many other more serious examples of price fixing in Japan.

Sources: "Wrapping Material Makers Face Charges over Price Fixing," *Japan Times*, October 1, 1991; "Wrapping Maker Admits Attending Price Negotiations," *Mainichi Daily News*, October 2, 1991; "Eight Plastics Producers May Be Indicted for Price Collusion," *Mainichi Daily News*, November 1, 1991; "JFTC Asserts New Muscle in Price Fixing Fight," *Nikkei Weekly*, November 16, 1991; Kazuyuki Fujita, "Court Slams Industrial Price-Fixing," *Daily Yomiuri*, May 22, 1993; Andrew Pollack, "Eight Firms Are Fined in Tokyo for Cartel," *International Herald Tribune*, May 22, 1993.

Hearing and reading these frequent reports, it is not surprising that "there is a strong belief in the business community in Japan that agreements to restrict imports, backed by threatened refusals to deal, are quite prevalent" (First 1986, p. 69). Two other phenomena that could be interpreted as manifestations of apparently widespread antitrust behavior soon become obvious to a newly arrived American executive in Japan: the disparity in retail prices between the United States and Japan, and the contrast between the enforcement practices of U.S. and Japanese antitrust authorities.

Prices in Japan

One of the basic premises behind fair-trade laws is the enhancement and protection of consumer welfare (Bork 1978, Graglia 1991). Japan's Antimonopoly Law declares one purpose of the law as being to "assure the interests of consumers." Consumer prices are frequently used as a barometer of consumer welfare. In fact, the basic proscription of antitrust law is that businesses should not have the power to enforce prices above competitive levels through collusion with competitors or exclusion of rivals (Krattenmaker and Salop 1987). Sustainable price differences for similar goods across different international markets have been recognized as a reliable indicator of nontariff barriers to free and open competition (Saxonhouse 1991). Lawrence (1991b) suggests that "if the Japanese market is contestable, we should see the potential for entry keeping Japanese prices in line with those of other markets" (p. 25). After reviewing his own data and many other comparative studies of prices in Japan (see below), and finding abundant evidence that prices in Japan are exceptionally high, Lawrence writes, "It is hard to understand, in the face of this evidence, how Japan could exhibit 'normal' import behavior when the evidence on differential pricing is so strong" (p. 30).

There may be many reasons for high prices in Japan. Two salient reasons that may have anticompetitive connotations are retail price maintenance and price-signaling practices. Examples are illustrated in Episodes 2.11 and 2.12, respectively.

Episode 2.11
High Prices in Japan— Retail Price Maintenance Practices in the Cosmetics Industry

For many years, cosmetics in Japan have been priced throughout the country at the manufacturer's suggested retail price, from the largest department stores to the smallest family-owned shops. Since 1973, Japan's Fair Trade Commission had approved retail price maintenance for 24 cosmetics items of ¥1,030 or less, but prices on thousands of cosmetics remained identical from store to store. In early 1990, a cosmetics retailer in Tokyo, Fujiki Honten, began discounting cosmetics from the manufacturer's suggested price. Soon thereafter, Shiseido, Japan's largest cosmetics company controlling more than a quarter of the domestic market and world-wide sales of ¥400 billion ($3.8 billion), suspended its contracts with Fujiki. Fujiki promptly filed a complaint with the JFTC alleging unfair business practices and violation of the Antitrust Law. In June the JFTC informed Fujiki that it would take no action because there was no evidence found to sustain allegations that Shiseido violated the law.

Fujiki then filed a civil suit against Shiseido in the Tokyo District Court in October 1990. During the court battle, Shiseido explained that the reason it had suspended business with Fujiki was that their contract prohibited retailers from any type of sales besides "face-to-face sales," a method Shiseido believes teaches customers the correct usage of its products and helps prevent skin trouble. Shiseido makes it a rule to sell its products by using sales clerks serving customers and explaining the products. The company adopted this sales method in 1923. Other cosmetics manufacturers immediately followed.

Fujiki President Ken Fujisawa submitted tape recordings of telephone conversations and sales vouchers as proof that he could buy Shiseido products by telephone from more than 10 department stores in Tokyo without hearing explanations from sales clerks, including products from The Ginza, a store directly managed by Shiseido. He also visited 43 Shiseido chain stores in the Tokyo area, actually purchased about ¥2 million worth of Shiseido products, and submitted the receipts to the court as evidence that several quality cosmetics were sold every five or six minutes without any explanation.

The suit was not concluded until September 27, 1993, three-and-a-half years after Fujiki first complained to the JFTC. The court found for the plaintiff, and ordered Shiseido to ship products to Fujiki. In the ruling, Presiding Judge Nobuo Akatsuka said Shiseido's chain store contracts restrict ways of selling and aim to keep prices at artificial levels without a rational reason. The court's decision was consistent with JFTC guidelines published in April 1991 regarding distribution and business practices that allow manufacturers to restrict the retail price of their products if they have a rational basis, but caution that if such restrictions create obstacles to fair-price competition they will be interpreted as a violation of the Antimonopoly Law. Under those guidelines, it became illegal to halt product shipments in retaliation for a retailer's price discounts.

Thus, it was rather surprising when in June 1992, more than a year after the JFTC published its guidelines on distribution practices, the JFTC once again denied a complaint from a cosmetic discounter, Egawa Kikaku, when Japan's second largest cosmetics maker, Kao, scrapped a contract with them. Egawa Kikaku also sued Kao in the Tokyo District Court. Yoshizo Egawa, president of Egawa Kikaku, submitted to the court taped statements by Kao executives that could be taken to mean that the cancellation of the agency contract was aimed at maintaining prices. Once again the court ruled in the plaintiff's favor and against the cosmetic company.

In 1993, the Ad Hoc commission to Promote Administrative Reform, an advisory body to Prime Minister Kiichi Miyazawa, urged the government to cancel the exemption from the fair trade laws allowing cosmetics manufacturers to dictate prices to wholesalers and retailers on the 24 remaining items. The commission's report concluded that the exemptions remain from a system created in the 1950s to protect and strengthen certain industries in order to prevent excessive competition. That spring the JFTC decided in principle to allow dealers to use their own discretion in selling cosmetics at prices lower than those recommended by manufacturers. Resale prices for 13 items were liberalized in April 1993, with the prices of the remaining items to be reviewed by the end of 1998.

On June 9, 1993, Kawachiya, another chain of cosmetic stores, began selling cosmetics at prices of up to 30 percent less than the manufacturer's suggested retail price. Kawachiya generally had a free hand on pricing because the products they offered were in the ¥2,000–5,000 range, but, like other cosmetics chains, they had traditionally followed the manufacturer's suggested retail prices. The new pricing affected about 5,000 items made by six leading manufacturers.

Within a few weeks, distributors for three of the largest cosmetic makers, Shiseido, Kao, and Kanebo, canceled contracts and otherwise restricted shipments to Kawachiya. The discount chain quickly filed complaints with the JFTC against all three companies for violations of the Antimonopoly Law, claiming that the companies were refusing to supply cosmetics in an attempt to prevent Kawachiya from selling below the recommended retail prices. The cosmetic makers charged that Kawachiya was selling their products at wholesale, making it impossible for sales clerks to give one-on-one counseling with customers, a "necessary" practice for health reasons. Yukio Higuchi, chairman of Kawachiya, said that Shiseido tried to persuade him to give up discount sales by offering ¥120 million as a sales promotion cost. Shiseido strongly denied offering money to manipulate business.

This time the JFTC responded more favorably to the retailer's complaint, and in July raided a Shiseido sales arm named in the Kawachiya case. In September the JFTC raided the headquarters and branch offices of three Shiseido wholesalers. And finally, on November 4, the JFTC raided Shiseido's headquarters looking for evidence of price fixing. Following a two-year investigation that expanded well beyond Kawachiya's initial complaint, the JFTC ruled in June 1995 that Shiseido had unfairly restricted retail prices by controlling the shipment of products to cosmetic discounters in violation of Article 19 of the Antimonopoly Law. According to the JFTC, Shiseido had repeatedly refused to allow Jusco Co., Japan's third largest retailer, to discount Shiseido products since the autumn of 1992. The JFTC found that in March 1993, Shiseido asked Jusco not to discount Shiseido products in exchange for product samples. Jusco decided to comply with Shiseido's request because it feared Shiseido would limit the amount of products available. After Kawachiya began selling Shiseido products at discounted prices, Shiseido executives visited major merchandise chains in June 1993 and asked them not to follow Kawachiya's practice, according to the JFTC. Daiei, Japan's largest retailer, still expressed its intention to discount Shiseido products, so Shiseido promised to that it would provide sales support if Daiei relented, the JFTC said. Daiei accepted because it also feared Shiseido would restrict deliveries. The JFTC investigation also revealed that a Shiseido-affiliated sales company concluded price maintenance contracts with 19 consumers' cooperatives in violation of the Antimonopoly Law. The JFTC demand that Shiseido stop such restrictions and that Shiseido

sales affiliates and consumers' cooperatives cancel the price maintenance contracts.

Shortly after the JFTC's ruling against Shiseido, the company submitted a report to the JFTC rejecting the JFTC's recommendation that
Shiseido stop imposing suggested retail prices on retailers because
they had never conducted such a practice. Shiseido acknowledged
violations of the law by signing resale contracts with consumers'
cooperatives, but said it could not accept the JFTC claim that it dictates
resale prices to retailers. The firm denied that it restricts shipments to
pressure retailers to sell its products at the recommended prices.
(Companies have the right to appeal JFTC recommendations to void
punitive measures and demand hearings, at which JFTC investigators
and company representatives argue the case before judges who include JFTC commissioners. If the company is dissatisfied with the
judges' ruling, it then has the option of filing suit with a high court.)

Another interesting twist to this case came in the autumn of 1993,
when an association of cosmetics retailers filed a complaint with the
JFTC against Kawachiya accusing the discount store of "dumping"
cosmetics on the market at 25–30 percent below prices recommended
by the manufacturers. For some products it is true that the discounters
were selling below "cost," but like many other industries in Japan,
cosmetic manufacturers have a rebate system in which the percentage
of kickbacks increases by volume. So even if a discount retailer were
to sell cosmetics at a "loss," he could still make a nice profit with the
rebates. The cosmetic giants fight this practice to protect the 200,000
cosmetics and toiletry dealers who are not large enough to offer
discount sales. Eighty percent of these stores are small "mom and pop"
outlets run by married couples. These stores cannot survive without
rebates and they cannot afford to discount.

Not to be outdone, six discounters, led by Fujiki President Ken
Fujisawa, formed an association of cosmetics discounters and asked
the JFTC to take stiff measures against the manufacturers. Because the
JFTC took no action in the dispute between Kao and Egawa (and
between Fujiki and Shiseido), Egawa asked the Tokyo District Public
Prosecutors Office to conduct investigations into suspected collusion
between the JFTC and the cosmetics industry.

It appears that the discounters are winning the battle. "Manufacturers are losing their grip on their distribution networks since they can
no longer force retail prices on retailers," said industry expert Toshi-
masa Tsuruta of Senshu University. Shortly after the JFTC's ruling

against Shiseido, Jusco began selling hundreds of cosmetics manufactured by Shiseido, Kanebo, and others at a 10–15 percent discount, marking the first time a major supermarket chain has launched full-scale discount sales of cosmetics. Then, in August 1995, Daiei cut prices of lipstick, eye shadow, soap, and other basic cosmetics by 15–25 percent. The tide has turned, and is highly unlikely to be reversed.

Sources: "Cracking the Distribution System: Kawachiya Challenges Cosmetic Giants," *Mainichi Daily News*, August 3, 1993; Kenichi Tsuruoka, "Kawachiya Battles Cosmetic Giants," *Daily Yomiuri*, August 5, 1993; "JFTC Challenges Cosmetics Price Structure," *Nikkei Weekly*, September 27, 1993; "Court Orders Shiseido to Ship Products to Retailers," *Daily Yomiuri*, September 28, 1993; Yukiko Matsuura, "Do Cosmetics Buyers Need Guidance?" *Nikkei Weekly*, December 15, 1993; "Cosmetics Makers and Discounters Squabble over Prices," *Yomiuri Report from Japan*, July 29, 1994; "Shiseido Discount Ban Illegal, JFTC Says," *Yomiuri Report from Japan*, June 22, 1995; "Jusco's Price-Cutting Move Has Cosmetics Firms Worried," *Yomiuri Report from Japan*, June 27, 1995; "Shiseido to Defy JFTC over Ruling on Pricing," *Daily Yomiuri*, July 3, 1995; "Battleground Shifts to Public Hearings as Shiseido Defies JFTC," *Yomiuri Report from Japan*, July 4, 1995; "Daiei to Slash Prices on Cosmetics," *Yomiuri Report from Japan*, July 26, 1995; and "JFTC Action Spurs Daiei to Slash the Price of Shiseido Cosmetics," *Japan Times*, July 27, 1995.

Episode 2.12
Identical Prices in the Beer Industry—Price Signaling or Competitive Pricing?

Within one week in March 1990, Japan's four major breweries all announced identical price increases on canned and bottled beer. It was the first time any of the breweries had raised prices in six years. Sapporo Breweries Ltd. was the first to announce the increases (¥320 for a large bottle [633 milliliters] of beer, up ¥20; ¥275 for a medium bottle [500 milliliters], up ¥15; ¥285 for a tall can [500 milliliters], up ¥20: and ¥220 for a regular can [350 milliliters], up ¥10), and within five days Japan's three other major breweries, Kirin, Asahi, and Suntory, all initiated identical increases. The prices announced are the suggested retail price, but nearly every retailer throughout the country sells canned and bottled beer at the suggested price whether the consumer buys one can or a six-pack (only a few discount liquor stores exist in Japan). Sapporo declared that the retailer would get 52.5 percent of the increase, the wholesaler's portion would be 21 percent, and the brewery would take 26.5 percent. Kirin, Asahi, and Suntory also decided to divide up the additional revenue in exactly the same proportions.

The four firms insisted that they had come up with the price hike decision independently of each other and that they did not discuss the price increases among themselves. Noboru Shimamura, managing director of Suntory, said the timing of the price increases was coincidental. Yoshinobu Takeda, a spokesman for Asahi beer, declared, "It just happened to be at the same time. This was based on our independent judgment." The president of Asahi, Kotaro Higuchi, clarified this by explaining that his company raised the price the same amount as the other three breweries to prevent confusion that could result if Asahi's increases at various phases of the distribution process were different from those of other companies. A spokesman for Sapporo beer commented, "We did it based on our own judgment, and we are not in a position to say why others did the same. But in terms of customer relations, I will say that if prices differ, it's harder to sell." One firm insists that its beer never be priced lower than that of a competitor because, the company believes, consumers think cheaper beer tastes bad. Asked why all four allocated the increase through the distribution chain in exactly the same proportion, the Suntory spokesman said, "That's something I shouldn't comment about."

Japan's Fair Trade Commission announced that it would question officials of the breweries on suspicion of colluding to raise prices. The JFTC pointed out that when prices of similar goods are raised by the same amount at the same time, it is assumed that the price hike was made as a result of prior consultations among companies, thus constituting a violation of the Antimonopoly Law. Tadao Shinjo, director of industrial investigations, said the JFTC could fine the companies if it found material evidence to prove that they discussed the price increase in advance among themselves. But he said the commission was investigating under a different provision of the law concerning concerted actions. No punishment would result, he said, but the JFTC might submit a report to Japan's parliament outlining the circumstances of the price increase. The commission ruled in 1980 and again in 1983 that the four beer companies had colluded to raise prices, but no punitive action was taken on either occasion. Following their investigation in 1990, the Fair Trade Commission announced that they found no evidence of a price cartel, but they asked the breweries to take actions to liberalize prices. In response, the four breweries placed a joint newspaper advertisement in October 1990 reminding retailers and consumers that "the price of beer is supposed to be set spontaneously by each store."

Spokesmen for all four breweries said they do not see much point in competing based on price. Toshihide Nattori, a spokesman for Kirin beer, said his brewery pegged its suggested retail price at ¥178 when the others raised theirs to ¥180 in 1975, but most stores just charged ¥180 anyway. According to a Tokyo Metropolitan Government price survey in January 1991, among the 132 convenience stores, 20 department stores, and 516 liquor shops surveyed, prices for bottled and canned beer were the same in almost 99 percent of the shops. Around 91 percent of 111 supermarkets surveyed sold beer at the brewers' suggested retail prices. But the breweries stress that the suggested price in no way prevents retailers from setting their own prices, nor are there rules prohibiting retail stores from selling goods at the suggested price. "We ensure that there is no kind of cartelization concerning the price of beer," an Asahi Breweries spokesman said. "Our prices are set independently. We cannot control the prices set by retailers. It is a matter for wholesalers and retailers," he said. One brewery believes that uniform prices benefit consumers because buyers "can only try various kinds of beer if each brand is sold at a level price." The National Liquor Retailers Union claims that if beer makers refrain from indicating their suggested retail price, consumers would be unable to "know the standard prices to compare and select products."

If consumers were upset by the uniform price increase, they did not show it. Japanese beek drinkers consumed a record 6.64 million kiloliters that year (1990), or 115 large bottles for every adult in the country. The Consumers Union of Japan has received few consumer complaints about the price increase. A spokesman for the Consumers Union explains, "We could see beer as a sort of luxury, and it could even be said that someone who has a complaint about the price of beer does not need to buy it. So it is not a problem that must be solved promptly."

Shinji Hashimoto, a senior official of the National Liaison Committee of Consumers Organizations, acknowledged that consumer groups do not have much clout in Japan. He believes the beer price increases are a typical example of a problem in Japan, namely noncompetitive price mechanisms. Hashimoto said stores legally have the right to charge any price they want for beer, "but based on the tradition of noncompetition, nobody does it." As a result, most consumers believe that beer prices are government regulated, he added.

The price of beer was controlled by the government until 1964, and some beer firms hint at the government's high liquor tax as a factor in the inflexible price system. About 44 percent of the price of beer is tax. "Beer sales serve as a source of a fair tax revenue," said Kensuke Suzuki, a spokesman for Kirin Brewery. "The government has been giving preference to stability in the beer market, eliminating excessive competition, to avoid a state of panic that might lead to a decrease in tax income."

If the government has contributed to the stability of high beer prices, it now appears to have hastened their decline. In the spring of 1994, Japan's four big breweries raised their suggested retail prices again in response to an increase in the government's beer tax (e.g., the price of a regular can increased from ¥220 to ¥240). Only this time, many large retailers fired back with price cuts. "We decided that we can't just keep going this way," said Isao Nakauchi, the chairman of Japan's largest chain of supermarkets. "It's a matter of how much influence is given to the makers." Daiei began selling domestic brands with discounts of up to 25 percent. Liquor discount stores like Kawachiya, who had "braved wholesalers' boycotts for years," grew rapidly and by 1995 controlled over 15 percent of the beer market.

An influx of lower-priced imports helped foreign beers double their market share in 1994 to 4 percent. Daiei began selling a Belgian beer named Bergenbrau for ¥128, nearly half the price of the domestic beers. The beer quickly became Daiei's best-selling beer nationwide. In early 1995 Daiei was selling 17 different brands of foreign beer at prices ranging from ¥128 to ¥158 per can. The Ito-Yokado group, owners of the 7–11 convenience stores, began selling Miller Ice Beer for ¥178. Jusco Co. and Seiyu Ltd. chain stores introduced other imported brands, with the former selling one brand at ¥148. In February 1995, Daiei put foreign beer on sale for ¥100 a can, and within a month sold 2.5 million cases. In an interesting twist to this story, within a month the Fair Trade Commission issued a strict warning to Daiei that there was a possibility that the beer sales may have violated Article 19 of the Antimonopoly Law, which prohibits dumping. Daiei discontinued the ¥100 beer, not because of the JFTC warning, but because they had sold as much of the discounted beer as they wanted, Daiei officials said.

Despite these pressures on pricing, Japan's four major breweries have yet to cut their suggested retail prices—and some say they will not. Instead, domestic brewers are trying to emphasize their superiority in quality over imports. "Imported beer, which is transported to Japan on ships over a period of several months, should naturally be lower in quality," said a spokesman for one major brewery. "I don't think imported beer tastes good. Consumers will eventually pay attention to this," claims Tsutomu Murai, honorary chairman of Asahi Breweries. "Japanese consumers are very picky in terms of the taste of beer," believes Yuzo Seto, president of Asahi. "They might try imports, but they will eventually come back to domestic brands."

Sources: "Asahi, Suntory Join Other Brewers by Raising Prices of Large Bottles ¥20," *Japan Times*, March 6, 1990; "JFTC to Quiz Beer Firms on Pricing," *Daily Yomiuri*, March 7, 1990; Fred Hiatt, "'Independent' Beer Price Hikes Under Fire," *Daily Yomiuri*, March 12, 1990; Satoru Nagoya, "Brewers Reject Charges of Price-Fixing," *Japan Times*, May 8, 1991; "As Japan Embraces Foreign Beverages, Local Retailers Lower Domestic Prices," *Asian Wall Street Journal*, January 9, 1995; "Imported Beer is a 'Black Ship' for Japan's Monopolized Markets," *Yomiuri Report from Japan*, January 25, 1995; and "JFTC Warns Daiei About ¥100 Beer," *Yomiuri Report from Japan*, March 23, 1995.

MITI (1992) conducted a survey of retail prices for a selected array of manufactured goods in Tokyo, New York, London, Paris, and Dusseldorf. Tires, cameras, camera lenses, floppy disks, video tapes, color TVs, VCRs, video cameras, and calculators made in Japan and exported to the United States were all more expensive in Japan than in the United States A joint investigation by MITI and the U.S. Department of Commerce (DOC) found that 42 percent of the made-in-Japan goods examined were priced higher in Japan than in the United States (Japan Economic Institute 1990). DOC and MITI also looked at relative prices in the two countries, comparing exact brands and models in similar retail environments. They discovered that two-thirds of the manufactured goods were on average 37 percent more expensive in Japan (U.S. Department of Commerce 1991). Another survey reported that Japan's retail prices were 48 percent higher than in the United States and 55 percent steeper than in Britain (*Economist* 1989). Japan's Fair Trade

Commission found prices for imported goods in Japan to be 80 percent higher on average than in their country of origin, although foreigners paid only 20 percent more for imported Japanese goods (*Economist* 1991b).

Saxonhouse (1991) questions the value of many of these pricing studies as simple tabulations from nonrandom samples. He cites an analysis (Cline 1990) of the determinants of the United States and Japanese prices differences found in the DOC-MITI study, in which Cline found no statistically significant difference between the U.S. and Japanese prices for Japanese-made goods, but did find a significant difference in United States and Japanese prices for goods made in the United States and Europe (Japan's prices were significantly higher). Saxonhouse argues that if the Japanese market were highly protected, "both Japanese and foreign products should have much higher prices in Japan than abroad" (p. 44). He suggests that foreign firms are attempting to maximize profits through low-volume, high-price sales. However, a random sample of exports from the United States to Germany and Japan, and German exports to the United States and Japan, showed that the exporters were not charging higher prices when selling to Japan, but that Japanese distributors were applying unusually high markups on foreign products sold in Japan (Lawrence 1991a). Trends in Japan's price indices support this (see Figure 2.2).

From 1985, the yen appreciated rapidly against the U.S. dollar, almost doubling in less than three years. This, of course, effectively cut the price of imported goods in half. Wholesale prices declined by 15 percent during the same period. Yet retail prices for Japan's consumers rose continuously (*Far Eastern Economic Review* 1989). Matsushita (1991) attributes this price rigidity, in part, to the control exercised by some distributors. In fact, Japan's Ministry of Finance announced that it would begin publishing monthly lists of "the actual import cost prices of major daily necessity items in an effort to pressure the importers into passing windfall foreign exchange profits on to consumers" (*Daily Yomiuri* 1993).

ANTITRUST ENFORCEMENT IN JAPAN

Anyone who believes Japan's AML has been violated can file a report with the JFTC. Following an investigation, if it appears that a violation of the law has occurred, the JFTC can issue a recom-

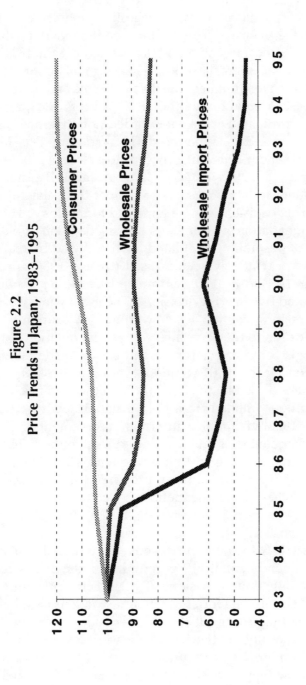

Figure 2.2
Price Trends in Japan, 1983–1995

Consumer Prices

Wholesale Prices

Wholesale Import Prices

mendation decision to the accused company advising it of the illegality of its behavior and suggesting appropriate corrective action. If the accused accepts the recommendation, the case is closed. If the recommendation is rejected, or if the JFTC believes it is in the public interest to do so, a hearing will be convened. After a hearing has been initiated, the defendant may admit the illegality and propose a solution. If the JFTC accepts the proposal, the hearing is terminated and a consent decision that incorporates the solution proposed is announced. If a consent decision is not forthcoming and the hearing proceeds to a close (a process that can take several years), the JFTC may issue a hearing decision ordering the defendant to take measures to correct the unlawful behavior. JFTC hearing decisions can be appealed to the Tokyo High Court.

Recommendation, consent, and hearing decisions are the formal methods of resolution stipulated in the AML. In reality, these measures are relatively seldom used (Uesugi 1986). In the eight years from 1984 to 1991, for example, there were just two consent decisions and five hearing decisions. The vast majority of cases are settled though a "caution" or a "warning." A caution is a private communication to the party alleged to be in violation of the AML; a warning is considered stronger and can be made public. Of the 1,114 cases closed with solutions between 1984 and 1991, 92 percent were settled by the JFTC through the issuance of a caution or a warning (compiled from JFTC Annual Reports, 1985–1992). Sanekata (1986) claims that informal enforcement is not uncommon in other countries, but acknowledges that the JFTC resorts to informal procedures much more frequently than do other countries. During the SII talks, Japan promised to make greater use of formal remedies. Recommendations have increased from 7 in 1989 to 22 in 1990 and to 30, 34, and 31 in 1991 through 1993 respectively (Richards 1993).

Japan's AML includes provisions for criminal sanctions, but since its amendment in 1953, criminal indictments have been issued on only four occasions. Two indictments came in 1974 against oil cartels, one for production restrictions and the other for price fixing (Ramseyer 1983). The production cartel was ruled to have acted illegally, but the defendants were acquitted because they had acted under the assumption that what they were doing was legal (because they were simply doing what MITI had told them to do). The defendants in the price-fixing case were found guilty, but their prison sentences were suspended. In 1993, eight plastic food wrap companies were found guilty of price fixing and sentenced to fines of between ¥6 million and ¥8 million (about $57,000–$76,000). Prison sentences meted out to the 15 executives involved were suspended (*International Herald Tribune* 1993). Also in 1993, the JFTC convicted four printing companies of fixing bids for a government contract to produce stickers for tax and pension notification postcards. The companies were fined ¥4 million (about $38,000) each, and executives were given suspended sentences (*Mainichi Daily News* 1993a). This case is presented in Episode 2.13.

Episode 2.13
An Antitrust Conviction in the Printing Industry

In the first convictions in nearly two decades under Japan's antitrust law, the Tokyo District Court on March 30, 1993, gave a former officer of Toppan Moore Co. a one-year suspended prison sentence, and a former officer of Hitachi Information Systems Ltd. an 18–month suspended sentence. Both men were put on three years probation.

The following day, at the request of Japan's Fair Trade Commission, the Tokyo High Public Prosecutors Office indicted Dai Nippon Printing (Japan's largest printing firm), Toppan Moore, Hitachi Information Systems, and Kobayashi Kirokushi on charges of bid-rigging. According to the indictment, the four companies held negotiations on April 22 and 27, 1992, regarding orders that the Social Insurance Agency was to place in May and September of the same year for the coded seals that the agency affixes to postcard notifications of pension payments. In the negotiations, the firms decided on one company that would receive the order and that this company would then subcontract the order to one of the other three firms. The companies agreed that the profits gained from inflating the prices of the orders would be divided evenly among them. The indictment charged that such an agreement violated Article 3 of the Antimonopoly Law.

The Tokyo High Court reached a decision in December 1993, ruling that the four companies had conspired beforehand to set an inflated price and to coordinate bids. The court determined that as a result of their illegal activity, the four firms had gained unjustified profits of ¥420 million. Presiding Judge Kazuyoshi Kondo said the firms "deserve severe social criticism" for causing heavy losses to the agency and the public. He added that bid-rigging has been widely practiced in the printing industry, noting that the four companies had been warned by the JFTC the previous year following revelations of bid-rigging on highway toll tickets. He criticized the four firms for ignoring the warning and continuing with their bid-rigging activity. The judge also chastised the Social Insurance Agency for aiding and abetting the bid rigging by its lack of strict oversight of the bidding process. The court fined each of the companies ¥4 million.

The JFTC ordered three of the four firms to pay a total of ¥170 million in penalties, but the firms protested and appealed the decision. The Social Insurance Agency asked the four companies to return the ¥420 million in unjustified profits, but the companies ignored the request. Dai Nippon Printing and Toppan Moore did, however, say they took the ruling seriously and introduced measures to ensure that such big-rigging is not repeated.

Sources: "Unusually, Tokyo Court Convicts Two in Antitrust Case," *International Herald Tribune*, March 31, 1993; "Four Firms Indicted for Rigging Government Bids," *Daily Yomiuri*, April 1, 1993; and "Four Printing Companies Found Guilty in Bid-Rigging," *Mainichi Daily News*, December 15, 1993.

In 1991, Japan's Criminal Code was revised to increase the maximum fine for bid-rigging from ¥1 million ($9,500) to ¥2.5 million ($24,000). In 1992, legislation was passed revising the upper limit of criminal fines for the offenses of private monopolization and unreasonable restraint of trade from ¥5 million ($48,000) to ¥100 million ($950,000). The fines assessed in the two cases settled in 1993 were at the minimum end of this scale. It remains to be seen if the JFTC will make use of these higher penalties.

In summary, although the AML stipulates penalties for violation of the law, enforcement appears to be very lax, raising legitimate questions about the law's effectiveness at deterring undesirable behavior. The main sanctions against antitrust violations are criminal penalties, but only the JFTC can initiate criminal prosecution for antitrust violations, and it almost never does. On the rare occasions that they take such action, the fines are relatively small and the jail sentences for executives are suspended.

By comparison, in the United States, criminal antitrust activity has, since 1974, been a felony offense with a maximum $1 million fine and a three-year jail term per count. Between fiscal years 1983 and 1992 the Antitrust Division of the Justice Department filed nearly 800 criminal cases and won convictions in 90 percent, resulting in fines of $206 million against 421 individuals and 726 corporations (an average of $38,000 for each individual and $262,000 for each corporation), and 237 individuals actually served time in prison for an average six-month term (U.S. Justice Department 1992).

An even greater fear and deterrent for U.S. businesses is the possibility of a private action filed by parties allegedly injured by anticompetitive behavior, in which the plaintiffs may sue for treble damages. Private actions have, since the 1960s, accounted for over 90 percent of all antitrust litigation in the United States, not without some questionable consequences (Baumol and Ordover 1985, Hills 1981, Neale and Stephens 1988). But in the more than 40 years since enactment of Japan's AML, private actions have been filed fewer than a dozen times, and only one has been successful (Haley 1982, 1984, Ishikawa 1989, Lipsky 1991, Ramseyer 1985, Sanekata 1986). Articles 25 and 26 of the AML allow for private recovery of damages, but stipulate that a tort claim cannot be filed unless and until the JFTC has issued a decision verifying that the conduct actually occurred and was a violation of the law (Baumol and Ordover 1985, Ishikawa 1989, First 1986, Matsushita 1990). Unfortunately for the plaintiff, as explained above, the JFTC resolves most of its investigations informally by providing a caution or warning to the accused, not a formal decision, denying the opportunity for an injured party to bring suit under the AML. The plaintiff could file a tort claim under Article 709 of the Civil Code (Matsushita 1993), but then the burden of proof lies with the plaintiff. Since cartels are not a per se antitrust violation in Japan, the plaintiff must establish intent to harm and actual damage. For example, a private damage case filed against an oil cartel was dismissed even though the existence of the cartel was confirmed because the plaintiffs failed to prove that kerosene prices would have been lower in the absence of the cartel (Ramsayer 1985, Toyama, Tateishi, and Palenberg 1983).

A myriad of other obstacles face a potential litigant (Haley 1978, 1982, 1984, Ramseyer 1985, Richards 1993). A court fee of up to 1 percent of the damages sought must be paid to the courts before the plaintiff can file a lawsuit. (From late 1992, the filing fees for civil actions with amount in controversy of more than ¥2 billion are to be reduced "approximately to half or less than half" (*Second Annual Report* 1992, p. 98). Class action lawsuits are not permitted. There is, by any measure, a woeful shortage of attorneys and judges in Japan, making it difficult to obtain representation, raising the cost thereof, and tying up cases in court for a minimum of five and up to 15 years. The JFTC and Japan's courts do not have access to the contempt power in order to enforce their decisions, and must rely on voluntary compliance or the threat of criminal proceedings. Until recently, plaintiffs have not been allowed discovery to obtain internal company documents necessary to corroborate their case. (As a result of SII, the JFTC announced that "copies or abridged copies of relevant decision documents are to be provided upon request by the injured parties" (*First Annual Report* 1991, p. 38). It has yet to be seen if this will result in a meaningful improvement in plaintiffs' access to critical documents.)

A provision for the assessment of surcharges was added to the AML in 1977. If an enterprise or association takes action that results in an unreasonable restraint of trade that effects the price of goods or services, the JFTC can order the offending operations to pay a surcharge equal to 6 percent (2 percent for retailers or 1 percent for wholesalers) on up to three years' sales revenues of the affected goods. These charges were increased in 1991 from 2 percent, 1 percent, and 0.5 percent respectively, due to pressure from the United States during the SII talks (the U.S. had asked for a minimum 10% surcharge). Excepting 1990 (during which a cartel of 12 cement companies was assessed a total surcharge of ¥12.5 billion), surcharges have averaged less than ¥2 billion annually from 1977 through 1991, an amount that is "trivial by American standards" (Lipsky 1991).

Japan's AML prohibits three categories of behavior: (1) private monopolization, (2) unreasonable restraint of trade, and (3) unfair trade practices. While the first two may also be considered "unfair," the distinction is important because the criminal penalties and surcharges available under the AML apply only to private monopolization and unreasonable restraint of trade, not to unfair business practices. There are, therefore, no criminal penalties or surcharges available as a remedy for unfair business practices (Haley 1984, 1991, Matsushita 1990). The only action possible is for the JFTC to tell the offender to cease and desist. There is no punitive penalty. The JFTC could bring criminal charges against an enterprise that fails to comply with JFTC recommendation, consent, or hearing decisions issued in relation to a case of unfair business practices, but this has never happened.

Law and economics literature regarding liability rules shows that higher sanctions cause individuals to avoid liability by reducing their level of activity and by increasing care (Snyder 1989, 1990). Regarding the relationship between penalties and control, Ramseyer (1985) summarizes current theory as "the optimal level of deterrence results when the burden to the wrong-doer of the sanctions for a given act equals the net harm which that act causes to other members of society, divided by the probability of the wrong-doer's apprehension and successful prosecution" (p. 605) or, in more simple terms, "smaller sanctions will in general fail to dissuade wrong-doers" (p. 606). As noted above, the probability of prosecution for anticompetitive behavior in Japan and penalties that would result are extremely low. "This dearth of enforceable deterrents . . . has led to exactly the consequences one would expect: a 'cooperative' economy characterized by widespread cartelization" (Ramseyer 1985, p. 637).

It is often claimed that there are few lawyers and lawsuits in Japan because the Japanese are a nonlitigious society who value harmony and compromise and avoid confrontation. Haley (1978, 1982, 1984) was the first legal scholar to look beyond this conventional wisdom. He found that the absolute incidence of litigation has been less frequent since World War II than during the years before the war. On a per capita basis, the rate of litigation had been more than halved. He attributes this decline to the inability of the legal system to provide effective relief due to the erection of a formidable system of procedural barriers by the governing elite. Meaningful access to the courts was restricted through bond-posting requirements, an insufficient supply of attorneys and judges, high costs, long delays, and other obstacles as noted above. Japan has fewer attorneys per capita now than in the 1930s (only 2.7% of applicants, about 700 people, are admitted to practice each year), and there are fewer judges per capita than in the 1890s. Haley (1982) laments, "What is remarkable about the Japanese legal system is not that people are reluctant to sue but that they sue at all" (p. 274).

Haley's work has been supported by Ramseyer (1985), who points out that "explaining the way people act as a product of their culture while defining their culture as the way they have learned to act" (p. 607) is faulty and circular reasoning supporting the claim that the Japanese are a nonlitigious society. He cites the writings of several Japanese scholars who found that the overwhelming reasons people in Japan avoid litigation are the high expense and the court delays. A distaste for litigation and damage to one's reputation were significantly lesser factors. Certainly, harmony and compromise are important Japanese values. But economics also plays a significant role. Japanese people sue less frequently because the cost is high, their probability of success is low, and the potential rewards are minimal. Ramseyer concludes:

> There are indeed few lawyers and lawsuits in Japan. This dearth has been a mixed blessing, however, for the scarcity of litigation has led to a substantial under-enforcement of the law. In antitrust, inadequate enforcement has resulted in price-fixing cartels and production constraints. This shortage of lawyers and litigation does not, as commentators have often suggested, result solely from a "nonlitigious" ethos. There may indeed be such an ethos, but it is an ethos buttressed by an array of institutional barriers to litigation that would discourage all but the most persistent plaintiffs in any society (p. 604).

Considering the evidence provided by Japan's price levels and the history of antitrust enforcement, the contention that anticompetitive behavior exists and acts as a deterrent to foreign imports deserves further examination. Further pursuit of this topic requires a brief review of the antitrust laws of the United States and Japan.

THE ANTITRUST LAWS OF THE UNITED STATES

The antitrust laws of the United States have their foundation in the Sherman Antitrust Act of 1890, the Clayton Act and the Federal Trade Commission Act both of 1914, and the Robinson Patman Act of 1936. The essential concern of the U.S. laws has been, from the beginning, the maximization of consumer welfare through the prevention of arrangements that increase market power without concurrently increasing social welfare by reducing costs or otherwise increasing efficiency (Bork 1978, Liebeler 1987).

The Sherman Act specifically forbids every contract, combination, or conspiracy to restrain free and open trade, but it was soon argued that the law was intended to punish only unreasonable restraints (Townsend 1980). In the *Standard Oil* case of 1911, the courts ruled that an act must be an unreasonable restraint of trade for the Sherman Act to apply. Toward this end, a distinction was developed between (1) cases in which a rule of reason should apply, and (2) cases considered to be per se violations of the law. Understanding that "both competition and cooperation must coexist in the economy in order for it to operate with efficiency and equity" (Murphy 1988, p. 44), the courts recognized that the legality of some competitive actions must be judged by the intent of the parties involved and the likely effect considering the market situation (Bork 1978). In these situations, such as refusals to deal and reciprocity requirements, a rule of reason applies and the case is judged by its own peculiar facts and circumstances. On the other hand, per se violations are automatically, regardless of circumstances, deemed unreasonable, unlawful, and incapable of legal justification. Per se violations are considered to eliminate competition without any chance of a corresponding increase in efficiency (Liebeler 1987). To gain a conviction for a per se violation, the plaintiff need not show adverse economic impact. In fact, courts have rejected defendants' testimony attempting to prove good intentions or good results arising from a per se offense (McAnneny 1991). Arrangements that have traditionally been deemed to be per se antitrust violations in the United States are bid-rigging, price fixing, boycotts, tying arrangements, cartels restricting output and/or supply, and division or allocation of markets by geography, merchandise, or customers (Ginsburg 1991, Graglia 1991, Murphy 1988, Townsend 1980).

The Clayton Act strengthened the U.S. antitrust arsenal by prohibiting trade practices that were not covered by the Sherman Act. It outlawed exclusive dealing and price discrimination. Both activities are subject to the rule of reason, that is, they are unlawful only if the effect may be to substantially lessen competition. The word "may," combined with the preamble's charge to "arrest the creation of trusts, conspiracies and monopolies in their incipiency," has led U.S. courts to judge "any imaginary threat to competition, no matter how shadowy and insubstantial" as reasonably probable of restraining trade (Bork 1978, p. 48).

Concurrent with the enactment of the Clayton Act, Congress also created the Federal Trade Commission (FTC) and empowered it to enjoin unfair methods of competition in commerce. Prior to the FTC, violations of antitrust laws were the jurisdiction of the Antitrust Division of the Justice Department. Since 1914, both organizations have pursued dual enforcement of the antitrust laws, with considerable—some argue inefficient—overlap (Gellhorn, James, Pogue, and Sims 1990, Nelson 1991). The Department of Justice focuses largely on criminal price-fixing and merger review. The FTC, which does not handle criminal cases, concentrates about 60 percent of its total resources on merger review (Nelson 1991).

In 1974 the Antitrust Procedures Act increased criminal antitrust penalties from the misdemeanor level with a maximum $50,000 fine and one-year jail sentence to the felony level with a maximum $1 million fine and three-year jail term per count. From 1970 to 1985, over 1,200 cases were prosecuted, nearly one-fifth with felony penalties (Snyder 1990).

The U.S. antitrust laws were originally and primarily aimed at domestic monopolies and cartels, although the act expressly extends coverage to commerce with foreign nations. In the 1940s, the prosecution of Alcoa (*United States v. Aluminum Company of America*, 148 F. 2d 416 [1945]) resulted in a clear extension of U.S. antitrust laws to activities of foreign companies even if those actions occur entirely outside the United States, as long as they have a substantial and adverse effect on the foreign or domestic commerce and trade of the United States (Simmons 1962, Townsend 1980, Victor and Chou 1985). Successful extraterritorial enforcement, however, depends on effective jurisdictional reach. Detecting, proving, and punishing collusion and conspiracy to restrain trade among foreign companies is extremely difficult. From gathering evidence to carrying out penalties, the complexity of nearly every aspect of antitrust litigation is compounded when prosecuting a foreign entity (Atwood 1984, Boudin 1990, Magney 1992, Neale and Stephens 1988, Townsend 1980). Issues of foreign sovereignty and diplomacy also complicate extraterritorial antitrust enforcement. If a foreign entity's actions are required by its own government, it is exempt from prosecution under U.S. law. Prior to the 1990s and the demise of the Soviet Union, U.S. trade and economic matters were typically a lower priority to defense and foreign policy concerns. This was particularly true with Japan. In nearly every major trade dispute over steel, textiles, televisions, semiconductors, automobiles, and so on, the Departments of State and Defense opposed and impeded retaliation against Japanese companies for violations of U.S. antitrust laws (Choate 1990, Prestowitz 1988b). A strong alliance with Japan and the strategic geographic military locations the alliance provided were deemed to be of more importance than unrestricted trade (Matsushita 1990).

The extraterritorial application of U.S. antitrust laws has recently been subject to considerably more debate. In 1977 the Antitrust Division of the Justice Department issued its *Antitrust Guidelines for International Operations*, which, consistent with the precedent established in the *Alcoa* case, reaffirmed that U.S. antitrust laws could be applied to an overseas transaction if there were a direct, substantial, and foreseeable effect on the commerce of the United States (Boudin 1990, Victor and Chou 1985). The Foreign Trade Antitrust Improvements Act of 1982 again reiterated this jurisdiction. There has been controversy, however, over the degree of U.S. commerce to which jurisdiction extends (Boudin 1990). The 1977 Justice Department *Guidelines* suggested that foreign anticompetitive conduct injuring U.S. commerce raises antitrust concerns when either U.S. consumers or U.S. exporters are harmed. In a 1988 revision of the *Guidelines*, the reference to exporters was omitted. Later, in 1992, U.S. Attorney General William Barr announced that Justice would take enforcement action against conduct occurring overseas if it unfairly restricts U.S. exports, arguing that anticompetitive behavior of foreign companies that inhibits U.S. exports thereby reduces the economies of scale for U.S. producers and indirectly affects U.S. consumers through higher prices than might otherwise be possible. Critics argue that comity concerns and the difficulties in gathering evidence and building a case around conduct occurring wholly within a foreign country make it unrealistic for the Justice Department to attempt such an extraterritorial application of U.S. laws (Magney 1992). Perhaps the gravest concern, however, is that the policy may lead to prosecution of foreign business methods that actually promote U.S. consumer welfare (Debow 1990), for it is predominantly believed in the U.S. economic and legal community that antitrust laws should be concerned solely with protecting consumer welfare (Bork 1978, Graglia 1991). U.S. public opinion has also traditionally and strongly supported the government's role as the champion of consumer rights against commercial interests. U.S.

antitrust laws have always reflected this grassroots backing. Such a tradition has not existed in Japan, and the development of antitrust there has been quite different.

THE ANTITRUST LAWS OF JAPAN

Following Japan's surrender and the end of World War II, U.S. occupation forces drafted and submitted to the Japanese Diet an antimonopoly law that was largely a composite of the Sherman and Clayton Acts. The Diet rejected the initial draft, and subsequently produced five alternatives (First 1993) until an acceptable version, the Act Concerning Prohibition of Private Monopoly and Maintenance of Fair Trade (hereafter referred to as the Antimonopoly Law, or AML), was adopted in 1947. Between 1947 and 1951 the occupation forces supervised strict enforcement of the law. But what was largely an American regulatory law was apparently ill-suited for the Japanese legal and administrative environment (Haley 1991). Sanekata (1986) declares that "the principles of competition policy . . . have never been widely accepted in Japanese business society" (p. 381). Within 15 months of the departure of the U.S. occupation forces, the AML was amended in a substantial relaxation of the original law (Hadley 1970, Haitani 1976, Haley 1991, Matsushita 1990, Nakazawa and Weiss 1989, Uekusa 1987). Cartels were deemed illegal only if they *substantially* restrained competition contrary to *the public interest*. Recession and rationalization cartels were exempted from the law. Mergers and acquisitions were more readily allowed. Resale price maintenance was allowed under certain conditions.

Enforcement was also relaxed. Matsushita (1987) describes the AML from 1950 to the mid-1960s as "dormant." During the occupation, an average of 27 violations were prosecuted annually. Following the 1953 amendment and through the end of the decade, the average dropped to six cases annually (Uekusa 1987). Writing about that period, Uekusa notes: "The Fair Trade Commission of Japan did not actively enforce the law in the 1950s because of pressure from business circles and the growing strength of MITI, which sometimes recommended anticompetitive practices" (p. 477). Sanekata (1986) is more diplomatic: "Considerable tension has existed between Japan's industrial policy and its legal commitment to antimonopoly enforcement. As a general rule, the interests of industrial policy have been preferred" (p. 379). One instance will serve as an example of the prevalent attitude. In 1957 the Diet formed a committee to consider further amendment (weakening) of the AML. After two years of hearings, the committee's recommendation included the following reasoning: "The regulation of the present Antimonopoly Act cannot necessarily be said to be most suitable for the proper operation of the economy of our country . . . (e)specially if we consider that the maintenance of the order of free competition as synonymous with the interest of the public should be judged from the higher standpoint of the producer, the consumer, and the economy as a whole" (Yamamura 1967, p. 75).

An important distinction between Japanese and American attitudes toward antitrust and the "interests of the public" is highlighted here. As noted earlier, it has long been the dominant opinion in the United States that antitrust laws should be used primarily to enhance consumer welfare, which has typically been defined in terms of price and preventing undue ability to control price. Yet there are some inefficient and wasteful consequences associated with this choice (DiLorenzo 1990, Ginsburg 1991). Bock (1981) suggests that the U.S. approach to antitrust is "something of a luxury . . . viable when the economy is sufficiently rich and able to afford it" (p. 7). To illustrate the point, she writes: "It is interesting to note that our economy has never resembled the Japanese economy so much as during war-time, when we permitted and, indeed, encouraged essentially association practices. During such periods, our economy has produced more output in shorter time spans at lower costs than ever before or since" (p. 7).

For the next two decades, cartels flourished in Japan (Dosi, Tyson, and Zysman 1989, Haitani 1976, Nakazawa and Weiss 1989, Uekusa 1987, Yamamura 1967, 1982). Recession and rationalization cartels were exempted by the amended AML. Recession cartels were granted to protect otherwise healthy companies from the strains of cyclical depressions. Rationalization cartels were permitted to facilitate an orderly transition and minimize social disturbance and hardship when an industry lost long-term competitiveness relative to foreign industries due to changes in structural factors. "Special cartels" such as small and medium business cartels, import cartels, export cartels and others were exempted through various statutes drafted by the Diet. Only Japanese manufacturers were permitted to join these various cartels (Fugate 1983). During the 1960s more than one-quarter of Japan's manufacturing was covered by over 1,000 legal cartels, about 90 percent of which were "special cartels" (Haitani 1976, Nakazawa and Weiss 1989). In addition to the legally authorized cartels, industries were often subject to administrative guidance from MITI which "involved something much closer to explicit cartel agreements" (Nakazawa and Weiss 1989, p. 642). Many of MITI's leaders felt that cartels were in the best interests of the nation, and by wielding control over import licenses, foreign exchange, low-cost credit, subsidies, and preferential tax treatment, they had the means to enforce compliance with their "guidance."

> Usually issued in the form of "non-compulsory" but nonetheless highly persuasive suggestions or veiled threats, administrative guidance is regularly used by MITI to orchestrate the unification of prices, the limitation of production, and, in some cases, outright cartelization (Toyama, Tateishi, and Palenberg 1983, pp. 601–2).

> The usual technique is for the MITI to announce guidelines for price increases, production cutbacks, or investment targets for an industry or for major firms. These guidelines are backed up by individual consultations with the representatives of the firms and trade associations. Explicit interfirm negotiations are deliberately avoided. The JFTC's reaction to this practice is one of reluctant acquiescence. The Commission admits that its jurisdiction covers only collusive actions among firms. It is powerless against collusive actions promoted by a government agency. It occasionally airs its frustration by issuing stern statements, pointing out that cartelization by administrative guidance violates the spirit, if not the letters, of the Antimonopoly Law. These warnings are politely ignored by the MITI (Haitani 1976, p. 134).

In 1980 the Japanese courts ruled that cartel-like arrangements formed under administrative guidance could be illegal even if MITI or other government agencies had recommended them (Ramseyer 1983, Toyama, Tateishi, and Palenberg 1983). The number of legally permitted cartels has declined since the late 1970s (Uekusa 1987), but "it would be difficult indeed for any objective observer to deny that the Japanese economy continues to exhibit 'collusive tendencies'" (Yamamura 1990, p. 37). As Yamamura explains elsewhere

(1982, p. 98), the prolonged procartel policy created an atmosphere where collusive conduct among firms was not regarded by some business leaders, even in principle, as morally or socially reprehensible. (See Episode 2.14 for an example.)

Episode 2.14
Cartels in the Cement Industry

Cement manufacturers, considered habitual offenders of the Antimonopoly Law, have taken a few tentative steps toward ensuring their activities stay within the limits of the law. In March 1991 the JFTC penalized the industry's biggest firms a total of ¥11.2 billion for organizing illegal cement cartels. But many analysts believe that the cement industry's distribution system will have to be improved if it actually intends to prevent a recurrence of its antitrust violations.

Following the JFTC's ruling, the presidents of the cement makers ceased their regular meetings, at least openly. But branch managers have held irregular meetings on several occasions since. The formation of illegal cartels by cement manufacturers stems in part from their close business ties with ready-mixed concrete suppliers, their downstream customers. One cement company executive commented, "Free competition needs to be promoted in the concrete industry if the JFTC wants to see it in the cement industry. But if free competition cannot be introduced downstream, then the formation of cartels in the cement industry should be allowed."

Source: Adapted from "Mitsuo Toga, "Cement Makers Chip Away at Illegal Cartel," *Nikkei Weekly*, December 28, 1991.

For the first time since its inception, the AML was strengthened through amendments passed in 1977 (Fugate 1991, Haley 1991, Matsushita 1990, Uekusa 1987). The legislation to amend the AML had been introduced in various forms since 1974, but sufficient support was not aroused until consumers became angry about petroleum cartel price fixing during the first oil crisis. The changes (1) authorized the JFTC to take measures to restore competition through divisions or divestiture in monopolistic situations (to this date the JFTC has never yet issued a divestiture order); (2) initiated a surcharge system designed to deprive cartels guilty of price fixing of the excess profits resulting from their illegal behavior; and (3) allowed the JFTC to demand explanations of parallel pricing when leading firms within an industry all raise prices by a similar amount within a three-month period.

More recently, the AML was influenced by the SII talks in 1990–1992 between the United States and Japan. The maximum fine for private monopolization or unreasonable restraint of trade was increased from ¥5 million to ¥100 million, and surcharges against price fixing were increased (*Final Report* 1990, *First Annual Report* 1991, *Second Annual Report* 1992). In addition, in 1991 the JFTC issued *The Antimonopoly Act Guidelines Concerning Distribution Systems and Business Practices* (hereafter, the *Guidelines*) to clarify enforcement of the AML (Lipsky 1991, Richards 1993).

The *Guidelines* describe more than 100 types of conduct that may be considered a violation of the AML, under 12 general descriptions: (1) customer allocation, (2) boycotts, (3) primary refusals to deal by a single firm, (4) restrictions on trading partners of dealing with competitors, (5) unjust reciprocal dealings, (6) other anticompetitive practices on the strength of continuous transaction relationships, (7) acquisition or possession of stocks of trading partners and anticompetitive effect, (8) resale price maintenance, (9) vertical nonprice restraints, (10) provision of rebates and allowances, (11) interference in distributors' management, and (12) abuse of dominant bargaining position. Of these, only customer allocation agreements and boycotts are described as violations "in principle" of the AML. The legality of the other actions depends upon their effect on competition in the market. The guidelines do not address price-fixing cartels, supply restriction cartels, purchase volume cartels, or bid-rigging, other than to note that these activities are, in principle, violations of the AML.

The United States continues to press for greater enforcement of Japan's AML, while Japan argues that the law and its enforcement have been enhanced and that the JFTC is vigorously eliminating anticompetitive practices (*Second Annual Report* 1992). Controversy remains around these two questions: (1) Do various anticompetitive behaviors occur more frequently in Japan than in the United States? and (2) Does the occurrence of anticompetitive behavior in Japan have a negative impact on the performance of American companies marketing manufactured goods in Japan? Based on the foregoing literature review, the following overriding research hypotheses are established:

H₁: Anticompetitive behavior occurs more frequently in Japan than in the United States.

H₂: Anticompetitive behavior in Japan has a negative impact on the performance of U.S. companies marketing manufactured goods in Japan.

OTHER COMPONENTS OF THE MODEL

To test the second hypothesis, anticompetitive behavior is introduced into a conceptual framework (Figure 2.1) consisting otherwise of components that have been studied repeatedly and that have consistently been shown in numerous instances to have a significant influence upon a firm's performance: characteristics of the market environment in which the business operates, characteristics of the firm and its competitive strengths, and the strategies used by the firm.

Characteristics of the Market

It is a well-established tenet within industrial organization literature that how organizations behave, the strategies they follow, and their ultimate performance are influenced by the environment in which they operate (e.g., Bain 1959, Bain and Qualls 1987, Craig, Douglas, and Reddy 1987, Lawrence and Lorsch 1967, Prescott 1986, Scherer 1970). As characteristics of the environment, these factors are generally beyond the control of management, although corporate decisions and actions obviously influence and shape the environment. The PIMS (Profit Impact of Market Strategy) data has shown that market growth rate, concentration among suppliers, inflation and unionization are aspects of the environment that have important influence upon profits (Buzzell and Gale 1987).

Price theory categorizes market structures by three general environmental criteria that have a significant impact upon performance: (1) the degree of seller concentration, (2) the extent of product differentiation, and (3) the condition of entry to the industry (Bain and Qualls 1987).

Entry theory (Bain 1959, Caves and Porter 1977, Johns 1962, Mueller and Tilton 1969, Porter 1978, 1980b, Shepherd 1979, Wenders 1971, Williamson 1963) explains how the structure of an industry can deter new entrants. Excess capacity enables the incumbents to engage in (or merely threaten) price warfare to dissuade potential entrants. Greater economies of scale can alter the cost structure and increase the absolute capital required to enter. Control over raw material or component supplies can create a formidable barrier. Product differentiation, research and development, proliferation of brands, and advertising can serve to reduce the cross-elasticity of demand between the incumbents products and those of the new entrants, thereby raising the cost of entry for a newcomer wishing to match or beat the status quo. Exclusive distribution channels and vertical integration can deny access and/or create efficiencies that could be difficult to overcome without a similar approach, again raising the cost of entry. In fact, it is the existence of such barriers that creates an environment wherein the performance of industry incumbents can excel (McWilliams and Smart 1993). If there were no barriers, new firms would continue to enter the market up to the point of long-run equilibrium, where above-normal profits would be eliminated. Of course, creating such barriers legally is what competitive strategy is all about (Porter 1980a), and preventing anticompetitive barriers is the purpose of antitrust and fair trade law.

It is expected that industry conditions such as profit margins and market growth rates will have a corresponding influence on the individual firm's performance. Characteristics of the industry that could serve as structural barriers to entry and expansion (e.g., market dominance by a few competitors, restricted distribution, limited suppliers) will have a negative effect on performance.

Characteristics of the Firm

Numerous studies have established the critical relationship between a firm's performance and its competitive strengths relative to competitors (e.g., Cook 1983, Day and Wensley 1988, Jacobson and Aaker 1987, Phillips, Chang, and Buzzell 1983, Porter 1980a, 1985, Prahalad and Hamel 1990). Porter's work suggests that success in any industry depends on the ability of a business to exploit its strengths through differentiation, cost leadership, or focus to achieve product or price advantages. Competitive advantage can arise from superiority in many different skills and resources: marketing, advertising, pricing, product differentiation, control of raw materials, research and development, innovation, sales force efficiency, service, quality, size, customer knowledge, and so forth. In fact, testing various hypotheses about which factors create the greatest advantages has been fertile ground for research across many business disciplines. Work based on the PIMS data base has provided a huge volume of empirical evidence of the links between various components of the marketing mix and perform- ance (see Kotabe and Duhan 1991 for a concise summary of 28 principles that have emerged from the PIMS studies, or for greater detail see Buzzell and Gale 1987).

Looking specifically at competition in international markets, size advantages, international experience, process innovations, and various product characteristics such as culture-specificity, strength of patent, unit value, uniqueness, age, and service/maintenance requirements have all been found to significantly impact perform- ance (Cavusgil and Nevin 1981, Cavusgil and Zou 1994, Douglas and Craig 1989, Kotabe 1990). Madsen's (1987) review of 17 empirical export performance studies found that factors related to product superiority (uniqueness, quality, design, pre- and postsale service) have a positive, sometimes very strong, effect on perform- ance.

Strategy

A relationship between strategy and performance, in both do- mestic and foreign environments, has long been postulated (Aaby and Slater 1989, Bilkey 1982, Buzzell and Gale 1987, Cavusgil and Zou 1994, Christensen, da Rocha, and Gertner 1987, Cooper and Kleinschmidt 1985, Phillips, Chang, and Buzzell 1983, Rosson and Ford 1982). Contingency theory has firmly established the principle that performance is contingent on the relationship between a company and its environment (Burke 1984, Glazer and Weiss 1993, Ruekert, Walker, and Roering 1985). An organization's strategies are the decisions and policies implemented by management that attempt to optimize the interaction between the organization's internal characteristics and the characteristics of its environment, ultimately affecting the organization's performance within that environment. It is the coalignment between strategy and the internal and external environments of the firm that is the key determinant of export performance (Cavusgil and Zou 1994). Inter-

national marketing strategies that contribute to successful performance require specific focus on, and adaptation to, local market
conditions, which in turn requires some degree of decentralization
and local decision-making autonomy.

The standardization of marketing strategies for global markets
has been much debated (e.g., Buzzell 1968, Levitt 1983, Wind
1986). The literature is reviewed by Jain (1989), who concludes that
the overall findings suggest that "standardization at best is difficult
and impractical" (p. 71). Samiee and Roth (1992) conclude that
"common views about standardization have rarely been supported
empirically" (p. 14). On the other hand, adaptation of marketing
mix variables to the local market has been shown to be an important
ingredient of success in foreign markets (Bilkey 1982, 1985, Cooper
and Kleinschmidt 1985).

To the degree that marketing mix variables must be adapted and
customized to meet local needs, tastes and competitive practices,
the required changes can be made better and quicker if decision-
making authority over such factors is decentralized with significant
local autonomy (Doyle, Saunders, and Wong 1992). Autonomy is
positively correlated with organizations that are flexible and effective in responding to environmental contingencies (Datta and
Grant 1990, Heflebower 1960). It is therefore expected that a
greater degree of local autonomy will have a positive influence on
the measures of performance success.

APPENDIX

Business Transactions in a Japanese Keiretsu:
A View from a Major Member Company

At a recent conference on Japanese business, several prominent
Japanese businessmen from a number of giant electronics companies affiliated with Japan's much-touted keiretsu, or industrial
groups, appeared puzzled by American academicians' perception
that the inner workings of industrial groups are nearly as cohesive
as those of the prewar Zaibatsu, the powerful financial/industrial
combines that drove Japanese business until they were dissolved
during the postwar occupation of Japan. The cohesive relationships
among member companies (i.e., a major bank, a major trading

company, and several major manufacturing companies) in a keiretsu are considered to have greatly contributed to Japan's dramatic postwar economic growth by dispersing risk through the accumulation of relationships to cushion shock in times of economic downturn as well as by establishing a virtual barrier to entry to Japan by foreign competitors (Saso and Kirby 1982, Nakatani 1984, Prestowitz 1988). The Japanese businessmen thought that our understanding of the cooperative nature of keiretsu arrangements was blown out of proportion. This led me to wonder why our perception, or understanding, differs from Japanese businessmen's.

Numerous books have been published on Japanese business management approaches and strategies in recent years (e.g., Prestowitz 1988b, Christopher 1983, Clark 1979, Davidson 1983, DeMente 1981, Gibney 1975, Kahn and Pepper 1980, Ohmae 1982, Ouchi 1981, Pascale and Athos 1981, Vogel 1979). These books and others have helped us understand the Japanese culture and language, and the historical development of Japanese businesses and industrial groups as well as their corporate strategies. In general, the development of industrial groups is considered to be rooted in such unique sociocultural factors as the vertical and group-oriented structure of Japanese society (Nakane 1970). Measures such as intercorporate shareholdings, interlocking directorates, and "old boy" networks of major university graduates are often used to demonstrate close working relationships within an industrial group. However, Japanese businessmen involved in day-to-day business deals both within and without their industrial groups see something different than those measures convey.

In this appendix, we will examine business relationships within an industrial group from the perspective of a member company's business transactions with other group members in order to bridge a perceptual gap between Japanese businessmen and American academicians. This will help us better understand the nature of Japan's industrial groups. First, the historical development and significance of keiretsu arrangements will be reviewed. Then, to illustrate business transactions within an industrial group, focus will be placed on a major electronics company considered to be a "star" company in an industrial group that grew out of one of the major prewar Zaibatsu.

THE ORIGIN OF THE KEIRETSU ARRANGEMENT

Until the end of World War II, the Zaibatsu had owned and controlled key industries including railroads, communication facilities, mining, and shipbuilding, all strategically important for Japan's push for industrialization. Strongly influenced by Japan's "trade-or-die" mentality, Zaibatsu-affiliated trading companies functioned as core trading arms for the Zaibatsu to sustain the lifeline of the burgeoning, resource-scarce Japanese economy by importing raw materials for manufacturing firms and exporting those manufacturers' finished products (Kotabe 1984).

Soon after the war, the Zaibatsu groups and their affiliates were dissolved by the Allied Occupation Authorities for two significant reasons. First, Zaibatsu-affiliated trading companies in close collaboration with other Zaibatsu members through collective decision making had served as a means of nationalistic interest supporting Japan's militarism during World War II. Second, the Zaibatsu had virtually monopolized prewar Japanese international commerce through their trading companies. However, because of a series of postwar political events, including the Cold War between the United States and the Soviet Union and the Korean War, the reunification of the Zaibatsu was implicitly encouraged by the Occupation Authorities as a means of mobilizing Japan's industrial resources to meet the supply needs of the Allies (Kojima and Ozawa 1984). The postwar Japanese government subsequently abolished the Occupation ban on intercorporate shareholdings and interlocking directorates and allowed a new form of alliances called keiretsu or industrial groups, to be formed.

The industrial groups that emerged from this reunification are more loosely affiliated than the original Zaibatsu. Each industrial group is led by a general trading company, a major bank, and a number of leading manufacturing firms. In contrast with the direct corporate governance of the prewar Zaibatsu component firms, family with thier close ties with the government, the postwar industrial groups have a more indirect means of coordination among leading member companies. Each industrial group has established a Presidents' Council, consisting of CEOs of member companies, which meets on a regular basis, both to socialize and to exchange ideas and informally discuss their corporate planning and coordination. Occasionally, government representatives from the Ministry of International Trade and Industry participate in an informal Presidents' Council meeting. Today, six leading industrial groups (i.e., Mitsui, Mitsubishi, Sumitomo, Sanwa, Fuyo, and Dai-Ichi Kangyo) alone account for about a quarter of the total assets and sales of all Japanese business corporations.

Therefore, the size and economic influence of these industrial groups are undoubtedly enormous. Their economies of scale in financing, production, and marketing and those of scope in pooling of technology and know-how form a formidable threat to foreign competition in Japan as well as abroad. To Americans, keiretsu arrangements are unfair, and thus are a form of nontariff barrier. In the United States, the Glass-Steagall Act of 1934 still prohibits bank holding companies from owning a commercial business venture (except for an international trading company involved principally in exports, thanks to the Export Trading Company Act of 1984), while the Clayton Act of 1914 prohibits certain monopolistic practices such as exclusive dealing, intercorporate shareholdings, and interlocking directorates. Not only are these practices common in Japan, but above all, they allegedly represent the crux of the inner workings of industrial groups.

If member firms in an industrial group do function as a collective organization for their collective good with a coordinated set of objectives, two inferences about Japanese markets could be made. First, it could be extremely difficult to establish a business relationship with any keiretsu member because of its tendencies to deal with other keiretsu members. Second, once a foreign company established a relationship with a keiretsu member, it should facilitate this foreign company's access to other keiretsu members for increased business (Coughlan and Scheer 1987).

If a keiretsu company sources a significant amount of raw materials and components from, and reciprocally sells its products to, other member companies, then a case may be made that the industrial group is insulated. If this is true, then it will be difficult for foreign firms to enter the Japanese market successfully without somehow aligning themselves with one or more of the industrial groupings. Often when foreign firms experience difficulty in developing ties with Japanese firms to gain market entry into Japan, they consider such industrial groupings a form of nontariff barrier (Lawrence 1987).

A CASE OF AN ELECTRONICS COMPANY IN A
VERTICAL KEIRETSU GROUP[1]

Takeshita Kogyo (a disguised name), founded in 1878, is a leading global supplier of a broad range of communications systems and equipment, computers and industrial electronic systems, and semiconductor devices, as well as home electronics products. With a total work force of 120,000, Takeshita Kogyo and its subsidiaries and affiliates operate 53 plants in Japan and 32 plants in 15 other countries.

Takeshita Kogyo is affiliated with the Maekawa Group (a disguised name). Typical of Japan's keiretsu, the Maekawa Group has major companies in such fields as banking, insurance, trading, steel, electronics, glass, oil, forestry, and metals, with overall group sales exceeding $200 billion. Some 30 percent of Takeshita Kogyo's stock is held by other Maekawa keiretsu companies, and Takeshita Kogyo returns the favor by keeping more than 35 percent of its own shareholdings in other group members. In addition, some 30 percent of its long- and short-term loans are provided by group institutions. These percentages differ for other companies, but the pattern is generally similar.

CEOs of leading companies of the Maekawa Group are represented in a presidents' council, called the "Hasu-no-Kai" (Water Lily Council), and hold regular meetings for purposes of social interaction and informal dissemination of strategic information among the member companies. A tendency toward group autonomy generally results in strong competition among industrial groups. Therefore, the Maekawa Group, like other keiretsu, attempts to have a strong position in every major sector of the economy. Since Takeshita Kogyo is viewed as a star high-technology company within the Maekawa Group, the company has been provided with financial as well as moral support by the group.

Takeshita Kogyo obtains various materials from and sells finished products to other member companies. These intrakeiretsu business transactions are shown in Table 2.1. Of its total materials purchase of $16.5 billion in 1995, Takeshita Kogyo's purchases from other member companies accounted for $0.3 billion. In other words, Takeshita Kogyo's intrakeiretsu sourcing ratio was merely 1.6 percent. Maekawa Trading Company was the most important materials supplier for Takeshita Kogyo. Although the breakdown

Table 2.2
Takeshita Kogyo's Business Transactions in 1995
Inside and Outside the Maekawa Keiretsu (in millons of dollars)

	Sales to	Purchases from
MAEKAWA KEIRETSU		
Maekawa Bank	14	0
Maekawa Metal	92	1
Maekawa Life Insurance	34	0
Maekawa Marine & Fire Insurance	29	0
Maekawa Trust & Banking	25	0
Yoshida Sheet Glass	16	3
Maekawa Chemical	15	1
Maekawa Trading	12	145
Maekawa Heavy Industries	10	35
Maekawa Electric Industries	9	47
Maekawa Cement	3	0
Maekawa Metal Mining	2	23
Other Member Companies	5	14
Total Transactions within Maekawa Group	365 (1.9%)	269 (1.6%)
Transactions within Takeshita Kogyo Group	19,112 (98.1%)	6,675 (40.5%)
Transactions outside the Groups		9,546 (57.9%)
TOTAL TRANSACTIONS	19,477	16,490

of original sources of materials purchased from the member trading company is unknown, the trading company's role as a materials supplier appears limited. Similarly, Takeshita's total sales in 1995 were $19.5 billion, of which about 0.4 billion, or a meager 1.9 percent, was accounted for by its sales to member companies. Maekawa Bank, Maekawa Metal, Maekawa Life Insurance, and Maekawa Trust & Banking have been considered the group's "key accounts" by Takeshita Kogyo and absorbed over 70 percent of its intrakeiretsu sales.

Despite the intercorporate shareholdings and interlocking directorates, among others, between Takeshita Kogyo and the rest of the Maekawa Group member companies, their business transactions have been insignificant. To further investigate this weak transactional relationship, Takeshita Kogyo's intrakeiretsu sales of computers was examined. Over the years, Takeshita Kogyo has focused its corporate effort on integration of computers and communications, and is increasingly well positioned to meet diverse needs in worldwide markets. Yet, Takeshita Kogyo's "key account" companies still heavily rely on IBM and other computer makers, while many other members of the Maekawa Group have adopted Takeshita Kogyo's computer systems. For example, Maekawa Bank uses IBM, NCR, and UNIVAC, among others, as well as Takeshita Kogyo's. On the other hand, Maekawa Metal and Maekawa Trust & Banking operate only on IBM computers. Despite the strategic importance of computers and communications business to Takeshita Kogyo, its computers have not become mainstream in the Maekawa Group, although there is always a possibility that they will. In addition, a number of member companies including Maekawa Life Insurance have established a consortium with IBM Japan to develop a new communications network independently. This further illustrates rather independent relationships among member companies within the same keiretsu.

All in all, it may be concluded that the Maekawa Group does not constitute any measurable barrier to entry by foreign competitors, barring the Japanese cultural tendency for Japanese companies to prefer domestic vendors over foreign vendors. Even this cultural tendency may be questioned on the basis of inferior quality of components and products from abroad (*Fortune* 1986).

WHERE DOES TAKESHITA KOGYO SOURCE THEIR SUPPLY OF MATERIALS AND COMPONENTS?

A keiretsu not only exists across industries (e.g., the Maekawa Group), but also exists within nonfinancial industries. A keiretsu arrangement within a non-financial industry is often called a "shihon keiretsu" (capital group) or "kigyo keiretsu" (enterprise group). A kigyo keiretsu consists of a nonfinancial parent company and a set of subsidiary firms tied by ownership, management interlockings, and credit policy to the parent (Hadley 1970). In a way, a kigyo keiretsu constitutes a vertically, yet loosely, integrated manufacturing network.

Takeshita Kogyo has its own vertically integrated group of affiliates. As of 1995, Takeshita Kogyo Group consists of Takeshita Kogyo as the parent company and a total of 94 affiliates (28 manufacturing companies, 31 software development companies, and 35 sales companies). What is intriguing about Takeshita Kogyo Group is the way its affiliates are formed. Although Takeshita Kogyo itself is an integrated electronics company, performing all manufacturing, software development, and sales within the company is not necessarily the most efficient and cost-effective way of doing business. There is a point in every aspect of productive activity beyond which diseconomies of scale set in (See, for example, Mallen 1973). Takeshita Kogyo has centrifugally spun off various activities when diseconomies have set in. As a result, Takeshita Kogyo has formed a consortium of specialized affiliates. Takeshita Kogyo's spin-off policy has solved the following two major problems:

1. Functional specialization is made possible for technical as well as cost efficiency.
2. Such resource bottlenecks as limited plant size and labor are reduced as spun-off affiliates have been relocated throughout Japan and abroad.

This spinoff-based integration contrasts sharply with integrations observed in the United States, which are based mostly on mergers and buyouts. It is natural that Takeshita Kogyo's affiliates are intimately linked to the parent company through interlockings of personnel and mutual trust as employees at the parent company have been spun off and assigned to affiliates.

As a result of this integration, Takeshita Kogyo has purchased $6.7 billion worth of materials and components from member affiliates of the Takeshita Kogyo Group. This internal sourcing amounted to over 40 percent of Takeshita Kogyo's total supply needs, worth $16.5 billion in 1995. Takeshita Kogyo's reliance on its affiliates for materials and components also has been increasing steadily over the years. One possible reason for increased reliance can be found in Takeshita's increased R&D intensity. R&D-intensive firms are likely to create an internal governance structure within the corporate system and internalize transactions involving proprietary knowledge and components to maximize value added by them (Buckley and Casson 1976, Dunning 1977, Williamson 1979). A second reason for internalization is the importance of the firm's internal management of the quality specification of components used for manufacture in order to retain the goodwill and confidence of consumers (Casson 1979). Thus, the more R&D-intensive the firm becomes, the more internal transactions occur within its integrated corporate structure.

In addition, loyalty of affiliates to the parent company is further reinforced by the just-in-time manufacturing system. The just-in-time manufacturing system often extends beyond the subsidiary line and includes a group of firms that have come to accept the leader company's goals as their own through socialization and compensation according to length of service and other nonperformance criteria (Ouchi 1980). It is also true with sales affiliates that organize distribution channels for Takeshita Kogyo's products. For example, Takeshita Kogyo sells about 90 percent of its semiconductor output through two captive distributors in Japan. Therefore, foreign competitors that are anticipating entry to or have already entered Japan face a formidable entry barrier, as they have to establish their own distribution networks.

Increase in internal transactions due to increased R&D intensity, the just-in-time vertical arrangement, and the captive distribution system, among others, are what foreign firms are afraid of as impenetrable competitive threats and also criticize as nontariff barriers to entry. However, they may not be considered either an unfair or illegal means of blocking out foreign competition. It is not simply because the same barriers face Japanese firms outside the arrangement, but more importantly because *they represent functional relationships that help reduce transactional uncertainty and opportunism among members, thus assuring mutual trust and efficiency* (Williamson 1979).

SUMMARY AND CONCLUSIONS

We have examined Japanese keiretsu arrangements from one company's perspective. Keiretsu exists in two ways: interindustry and intraindustry. Maekawa Group is an interindustry keiretsu, of which Takeshita Kogyo is a member. Takeshita Kogyo itself has its own vertically arranged intraindustry kigyo keiretsu, or enterprise group of firms functionally related along the value added chain.

Although reminiscent of prewar Zaibatsu in the form of inter-corporate shareholdings, interlocking directorates, and an "old boy" network of major university graduates, an interindustry keiretsu appears to have lost substance to a much larger extent than is commonly thought. As one Japanese businessman admits, "higoro no kankei" (literally, daily relationships implying golfing and social drinking, as well as high-level Presidents' Council meetings) somewhat facilitates business relations among member companies, but constitutes little more than neighborly friendship.

We have shown that vertically arranged enterprise groups, such as Takeshita Kogyo Group, have become more significant in Japan. An enterprise group is made up mostly of component affiliate firms that have been spun off from a parent company and companies have come into long-term working relationships so as to achieve economies of scale through specialization. This type of vertical integration (more aptly, vertical disintegration-cum-reintegration) contrasts sharply with those observed in the United States through buyouts and mergers. Long-term working relationships and resultant strong mutual trust are more likely to emerge in Japan's enterprise groups than in vertically integrated companies in the United States.

This enterprise group arrangement may form an invincible barrier to foreign competitors entering Japanese markets, since it literally controls all phases of the value-added chain from components sourcing to manufacturing to distribution.[2] The importance of attaining competitive strength in various phases of the value-added chain has been well documented elsewhere (Kogut 1985, Porter 1986, Robinson 1987). Japanese firms have started extending their enterprise group strategy to foreign markets, as exemplified by Japanese suppliers of automobile components investing in the United States to follow Japanese auto manufacturers operating in

the United States. This is one of the sources of Japanese competitiveness, both in Japan and abroad.

NOTES

1. Data are all disguised to assure confidentiality. Disguised values
shown here are derived by multiplying real values by a certain common
factor so as to preserve ratios. For example, Company A's sale to
Companies B and C of $10 million and $5 million, respectively, might be
represented by multiplying these values by a common factor of .8. The
reported data would then show sales of $8 million and $4 million,
respectively. This system of computation preserves all ratios in that
Company A sold twice as much to Company B as to Company C.

2. A good example of a European enterprise group is Benetton Spa of
Italy, for which much of the above discussion holds. Benetton owns or
strongly influences the value chain, from knitting to retailing of sweaters
and other clothes. In this respect, Italy is becoming known as the "Japan
of Europe."

3

Research Design and Methodology

As far as the preceding literature review could determine, amidst all of the claims and counterclaims regarding the occurrence of anticompetitive behavior in Japan and the inadequate enforcement of the Antimonopoly Law, empirical investigation of the specific types of alleged collusive anticompetitive practices is nonexistent. Ryans's (1988) literature review discovered no empirical research directly examining the impact of nontariff barriers on market share achievement. Ryans's own research tested the impact of nontariff barriers in general by asking respondents to indicate on a seven-point scale the extent to which market penetration had been slowed by "nontariff barriers." No specific barriers or anticompetitive practices were described or investigated. In his study of extraterritorial antitrust, Townsend (1980) found American business executives extremely reluctant to talk openly about antitrust issues. When the United States designated Japan as an unfair trading nation under Section 301 of the Omnibus Trade Act and began investigating barriers to wood products, supercomputers, and satellites, not a single U.S. business in those industries, not even those that had privately requested government action, would go public with specific examples of anticompetitive practices (Rockwell 1989).

This paucity of research and the reluctance of business executives to go public with specific accusations is understandable. As noted earlier, in an environment where the probability of successful prosecution is low, and the negative consequences could be high (including the possibility of alienation and retaliation from the local industry and bureaucracy), maintaining silence and attempting simply to work within the system may be the most reasonable course of action. Therefore, considering the difficulties of collecting data concerning such a sensitive topic, a research instrument was designed that would allow respondents to indicate the relative occurrence of various anticompetitive activities and their impact, without disclosing specific information about the parties involved.

RESEARCH OBJECTIVES

The purpose of the research is to answer two overriding questions: (1) Do various anticompetitive behaviors occur more frequently in Japan than in the United States? and (2) Does the occurrence of anticompetitive behavior in Japan have a negative impact on the performance of American companies marketing manufactured goods in Japan? This study will go beyond an investigation of barriers in general, and will look at specific types of anticompetitive activities as defined and prohibited by Japan's Antimonopoly Law.

Answers to these questions, or at least additional understanding, can be of immediate use to U.S. and Japanese government policy makers, trade negotiators, and law enforcement officials. As far as business practitioners are concerned, if anticompetitive behavior does impact the ability of U.S. manufacturers to enter Japanese markets, energy can be focused on particular measures to eliminate or reduce the practices and their consequences. If such behavior is found to be absent, or to have few real business repercussions, American businesses can forge ahead with market entry and expansion efforts in Japan without undue distraction caused by perceived concerns about anticompetitive barriers. If a particular behavior occurs with similar frequency in Japan as in their home market, U.S. companies could still be justified in calling for better law enforcement, but the activity's classification as a Japanese barrier to foreign imports would be more difficult to justify.

THE RESEARCH INSTRUMENT

Considering the difficulties of collecting data concerning such a sensitive topic, a research instrument was designed that would allow respondents to indicate the relative occurrence and impact of various anticompetitive activities without disclosing specific information about the parties involved. This was done by inquiring into the occurrence of specific activities which are, in principle, violations of Japan's antimonopoly law, relative to their practice in the United States. Ten specific examples of anticompetitive behavior were selected from the Japanese FTC *Guidelines*. While the anticompetitive nature of the action may have been obvious, during the data collection the descriptive word anticompetitive was never used. Rather, the ten scenarios were referred to as "possible types of competitive behavior," with no judgment of fairness or legality implied. Respondents were asked to indicate on a 5-point scale of "Much Less Often" to "Much More Often" the frequency of occurrence in Japan of the described behavior relative to occurrence in the United States The midpoint of the scale indicated that the relative frequency is the same, without specifying the rate of occurrence (i.e., if the behavior is widespread in both markets or does not occur at all in both markets, the appropriate response in either case would be at the midpoint of the scale). By investigating the relative frequency of occurrence rather than the actual rate of occurrence, respondents could provide data regarding the extent of the problem without divulging sensitive information. Even when indicating that the behavior occurs more or less in one market or the other, executives were not required to identify the practicing parties or provide further detail. Only the issues of frequency of occurrence and impact on performance were queried.

Prior to answering any questions, all respondents were asked to identify one business unit within their organization having considerable long-term significance to their company's objectives in Japan, and respond to all questions in reference to that business line only. This was intended to avoid what has been a methodological weakness in some studies of export performance that have collected data at the overall company level (Cavusgil and Zou 1994,

Madsen 1987). Conditions, practices, and performance can vary widely across various product-market export ventures of the same firm. Investigating at the overall firm level can result in confounded findings. Export success can be more accurately analyzed at the product level rather than the enterprise level (Cavusgil and Kirpalani 1993).

There is clear evidence that formal barriers to imports have been reduced and the degree of access to markets in Japan has improved (ACCJ 1991, McKinney 1989). The government of Japan has officially recognized "the necessity to enhance the overall deterrent effect against antimonopoly violations" (*Second Annual Report* 1992, p. 96) and, since 1989, has taken some steps to enhance enforcement of the AML such as increasing the maximum allowable surcharges and criminal fines, as noted earlier. This research was, therefore, designed to measure the effect of current anticompetitive activities on recent performance (the past three years), and does not attempt to investigate the influence of currently defunct behaviors or policies that may have historically served as market barriers.

SAMPLE

To investigate the occurrence of anticompetitive behavior in Japan relative to the United States, and the effect on U.S. business efforts to market manufactured goods in Japan, information was solicited from U.S. companies that are actually doing business in Japan and have advanced sufficiently in their commitment, development, and experience that they have established their own offices and operations in Japan. The U.S. Department of Commerce reports that almost 85 percent of total exports of manufactured goods from the United States come from about 250 firms, most of which are multinationals on the Fortune 500 list of industrial corporations (U.S. Department of Commerce 1987). About 220 of the Fortune 500 industrials have a business presence in Japan (Allen 1994). Using the 1993 membership directory of the American Chamber of Commerce in Japan, 187 Fortune 500 companies were identified. An additional eight private companies of similar size, also ACCJ members, were added to the sample. The "company voting" member, in almost every case the highest ranking officer in Japan, was targeted for contact. Thus, the entire sample consists of U.S. manufacturing companies that have established a physical presence and a workforce in Japan. These are organizations that have made a significant commitment to do business in Japan and backed it up with a substantial investment. Agents, distributors, or other third-party representatives of U.S. companies were not included in the sample.

It is highly probable that there are American companies that attempted to operate in Japan but were unsuccessful due to genuine anticompetitive barriers. Obtaining relevant information from these companies would be pertinent and useful to this investigation, but identifying such companies from among the total population of U.S. companies that are not marketing products in Japan would be difficult and inefficient. Even if such companies could be found, their experience with anticompetitive behavior in Japan may no longer be timely, and may have been limited in scope. Surveying large U.S. companies operating in Japan assures that the collected data will reflect the current situation as perceived by executives "in the field."

It is also possible that some U.S. companies have not attempted to enter the Japanese market because of what they perceive to be an insurmountable level of anticompetitive activity. Considering the frequently voiced allegations against Japan's supposedly unfair trade practices, it is conceivable that such claims alone could act as a deterrent to new entrants. Managerial decisions are driven by perceptions (Einhorn and Hogarth 1981, March 1978, Slovic, Fischhoff, and Lichtenstein 1977), perceived barriers influence executives' marketing decisions (Karakaya and Stahl 1989), and nonexporters have been found to perceive export barriers as more formidable obstacles than is actually the case for those who are exporting (Kedia and Chokar 1986). However, even if such companies were identified, their opinions and perceptions would not be germane to the questions addressed in this study concerning the relative rate of occurrence of anticompetitive behavior in Japan and its impact on business performance. American bureaucrats and businessmen who have not actually operated in Japan over an extended period would lack the first-hand experience required to respond knowledgeably.

Japanese companies, whether operating in Japan or the United States, were not included in the survey for several reasons. It is unlikely that executives of Japanese companies working in Japan would be sufficiently familiar or experienced with American business practices, U.S. antitrust law, and its enforcement to render a valid opinion on the relative occurrence of anticompetitive behavior in the two countries. Japanese executives would be knowledgeable about the absolute rate of occurrence in Japan, but asking about absolute occurrence requires the disclosure of sensitive information, which the questionnaire was specifically designed to avoid in order to improve the probability of response. Even if the executives would provide such sensitive data, it is unlikely they could say in absolute numbers how often a particular activity occurs. Their point of reference must of necessity become relative to something else. For any particular industry in Japan, the relative rate of anticompetitive behavior could be quite different if compared to other industries in Japan rather than the same industry in the United States.

Japanese executives working as expatriates in America would be capable of expressing an opinion regarding the relative occurrence of anticompetitive behavior in the two countries, but they would not be able to provide information about the impact of anticompetitive behavior on U.S. business performance in Japan. They would know about the impact on Japanese business performance in the U.S., but that is neither a trade issue nor an inquiry of this study. Japan has accused the United States of multiple unfair trade practices, and, in fact, declared America to be the worst offender among all of Japan's trade partners (*Far Eastern Economic Review* 1992), charging the United States with violations, abuses, and misuses of GATT provisions, restrictions on services trade, deficiencies in intellectual property protection, and various unilateral actions such as the extraterritorial application of U.S. antitrust law. But anticompetitive behavior in the United States and lax enforcement of U.S. antitrust law, have not been trade issues raised by the Japanese, and the value of soliciting such information would be questionable.

Although data were collected exclusively from executives of U.S. companies, this does not imply that only Americans responded. Many U.S. companies' Japan operations are led by executives who are Japanese citizens or other nationalities. As will be discussed later, one-half of the respondents were not American citizens.

The assistance of an American business executive in Tokyo was solicited to encourage participation with the study. This executive has lived in Japan for more than ten years, managed his company's business there for twenty years, served two terms as the president of the ACCJ, was on the ACCJ Board of Governors at the time of the survey, and is well known and respected in the Tokyo business community. He mailed a letter to each of the 195 executives in the sample, which informed them of the impending study, introduced the researchers, and requested cooperation with the study. To minimize a potential response bias, the executive's letter provided only a brief description of the study, stating simply that the research would be "an examination of how the market environment in Japan affects the strategies and performance of U.S. companies doing business in Japan."

The American executive's message was followed by a letter from the researchers explaining the study and notifying the executives that they would be called within a few days to arrange for an appointment. Each executive then received a personal call requesting his or her cooperation. Those that agreed to participate in the study were given three response options: (1) mail questionnaire, (2) telephone interview, or (3) personal interview. In all three cases, an identical data collection instrument was used. Mail questionnaires included a stamped return envelope and a cover letter with instructions. The same instructions were relayed verbally during the telephone and personal interviews. All of the telephone and personal interviews were conducted by the authors in Japan. Due to the sensitive nature of some of the questions, and because the respondents were promised complete confidentiality, the mail questionnaires were returned directly to the authors. All responses were encoded and input completely and solely by the authors. A copy of the survey instrument is presented at the end of the book.

PROFILE OF THE RESPONDENTS

Responses were received from 131 of the companies contacted. Two of the responses were unusable (the respondents, both Japanese, reported that they had no domestic competition for the products they were selling in Japan), resulting in 129 usable responses from a sample of 195, an effective response rate of 66.2%. It is believed that the high response rate was due to a combination of factors, most notably (1) the involvement of the U.S. business executive mentioned above (several respondents told the authors that had it not been for the executive's introduction, they would not have responded); (2) genuine interest among the business community in the research issue and a desire to cooperate with efforts that may help to improve the U.S.–Japan trade relationship (86 percent of the respondents requested a summary report of the research findings); (3) the combination of both mail and telephone contact prior to receiving the questionnaire; (4) three response options (mail, telephone, or personal interview); and (5) the authors' actual travel to Japan to conduct the data collection.

Because of the high response rate, and the frequency of contact preceding the study, multiple mailings were not utilized. Respondents who agreed to complete a mailed questionnaire but did not return the data were not contacted again. The most frequently cited reason for nonparticipation was that the executive would be traveling outside Japan during the time that the authors would be in Japan collecting data (two- to three-week business trips are not uncommon for U.S. expatriate executives). Information about the respondents and their companies is summarized in Tables 3.1 through 3.8.

As shown in Table 3.1, approximately two-thirds of the respondents used the mail questionnaire, 22 percent were interviewed via telephone, and the balance (14 percent) were personally interviewed in their Tokyo offices. An analysis of variance (ANOVA) was performed to test for significant differences in response patterns considering data collection methodology. In no case were responses on the mail questionnaires (64 percent of the total) significantly different from the responses recorded in the telephone and personal interviews. There were three cases where response patterns varied between telephone and personal interviews, but these differences followed no consistent pattern and no logical explanation

Table 3.1
Method of Data Collection

Technique Used	Number of Responses	Percent of Total
Mail Questionnaire	83	64.3%
Telephone Interview	28	21.%
Personal Interview	18	14.0%
Total	129	100.0%

could be conceived to explain the variation other than an aberration due to the fewer number of personal interviews (14 percent of the total responses). To check the impact upon the analysis reported in Chapter 4, the same procedures were repeated excluding the data received via personal interviews. The results were very similar, with no meaningful change in the outcome or the significant variables.

The breakdown of respondents' nationalities and the length of their job experience is presented in Tables 3.2, 3.3, and 3.4. One-half of the respondents were Americans, 70 percent of whom have been with their current company for more than 10 years (39 percent have more than 20 years experience with the same company). Almost two-thirds of the American executives, 61 percent, have been involved with their company's Japan business for more than five years (28 percent have more than 10 years experience with their business in Japan). Thirty-nine percent of the respondents were Japanese. As would be expected, these executives have

Table 3.2
Nationality of Respondents

Nationality	Number of Responses	Percent of Total
American	64	49.6%
Japanese	50	38.8%
Other	15	11.6%
Total	129	100.0%

Table 3.3
Respondents' Years of Experience with Company

Nationality	0–5	6–10	11–15	16–20	More than 20
American	13	6	12	8	25
Japanese	15	11	5	4	15
Other	1	2	4	3	5
Total	29	19	21	15	45
% of Total	22.5%	14.7%	16.3%	11.6%	34.9%

Table 3.4
Respondents' Years of Experience Working in Japan

Nationality	0–5	6–10	11–15	16–20	More than 20
American	25	21	7	2	9
Japanese	4	8	1	6	31
Other	12	2	1	0	0
Total	41	31	9	8	40
% of Total	31.8%	24.0%	7.0%	6.2%	31.0%

much more experience working in Japan (nearly two-thirds have greater than 20 years experience). About one-half have been employed with their current company for more than 10 years. Fifteen executives of other nationalities (e.g., Canada, Australia, and various European countries) accounted for 11.6 percent of the respondents, most (80 percent) of whom have been working for the same company for at least the past 10 years, and all but three of whom have been involved with their company's business in Japan for less than five years.

An analysis of variance was performed to test for significant differences in response patterns by nationality of respondents. Japanese and American executives did vary considerably in their assessment of the occurrence of anticompetitive behavior in Japan relative to its occurrence in the United States (i.e., Americans believe it occurs more often while Japanese do not). This is an important finding and will be discussed at length in the following chapter. The only other significant difference in response patterns by nationality was that Japanese respondents rated their company's economies of scale and bargaining position with customers as being stronger relative to competitors than did Americans or executives of other nationalities. This optimism was not, however, repeated in other assessments of company strength regarding the company's products and service.

As shown in Table 3.5, the responding companies represent 24 general industries (industries with three or fewer respondents are aggregated in "Other"). No single industry accounts for more than 11 percent of the data. (Because executives were asked to respond

Table 3.5
Industrial Classification of Responding Companies

Industry	Number of Responses	Percent of Total
Chemicals	14	10.9%
Computers & Office Equipment	14	10.9%
Electronics & Electrical Equipment	14	10.9%
Food	9	7.0%
Forest Products	8	6.2%
Industrial & Farm Equipment	6	4.7%
Metals & Metal Products	7	5.4%
Motero Vehicles & Parts	9	7.0%
Petroleum Refining	4	3.1%
Pharmaceuticals	8	6.2%
Scientific & Photo Equipment	11	8.5%
Soaps & Cosmetics	4	3.1%
Other	21	16.3%
Total	129	100.0%

in reference to only one business unit of their company, it is possible, for example, that an organization that is classified in *Fortune* as an aerospace or computer company may have chosen to respond in reference to its scientific equipment or metal products or auto parts operations in Japan, thereby putting that company in a different industrial classification than it might appear in in other publications.) Table 3.6 shows that about two-thirds (62.8 percent) of the companies responded in reference to industrial products, while the balance were marketing consumer goods.

Considering that the sample consists of Fortune 500 companies, the breakdown shown in Table 3.7 comes as no surprise. These are large organizations: only 16.3 percent had total worldwide sales of less than $1 billion in 1993, and half had sales in excess of $5 billion. Table 3.8 confirms that these companies have a considerable amount of experience in Japan. Over half (53.5 percent) have operated there for more than 20 years.

Table 3.6
Classification of Product Type

Product Type	Number of Responses	Percent of Total
Consumer Goods	48	37.2%
Industrial Goods	81	62.8%
Total	129	100.0%

Table 3.7
Total 1993 Worldwide Sales Revenue of Responding Companies

1993 Sales Revenue	Number of Responses	Percent of Total
Less than $1 billion	21	16.3%
$1–$4.99 billion	45	34.9%
$5–$9.99 billion	28	21.7%
$10–$19.99 billion	14	10.9%
More than $20 billion	16	12.4%
No Responses	5	3.9%
Total	129	100.0%

Table 3.8
Responding Companies' Years of Operating Experience in Japan

Years in Japan	Number of Responses	Percent of Total
0–5 years	16	12.4%
6–10 years	19	14.7%
11–15 years	9	7.0%
16–20 years	15	11.6%
More thatn 20 Years	69	53.5%
No Responses	1	0.8%
Total	129	100.0%

OPERATIONALIZATION OF THE VARIABLES

The Occurrence of Anticompetitive Behavior

The method used to collect information regarding the relative occurrence of anticompetitive behavior was briefly described earlier. Japanese newspaper articles related to anticompetitive practices were scanned to compile an initial list of apparent activities. These were then compared with information contained in the JFTC Guidelines, resulting in ten specific descriptions of anticompetitive behavior that are violations, in principle, of Japan's AML. (Whether the activity is actually a violation of the law would depend upon the impact upon competition, which would have to be determined by an JFTC investigation of the specific circumstances surrounding each case.) The ten scenarios are:

1. *Refusal to Supply*: A manufacturer informs independent distributors or end users that the manufacturer will not supply products if the distributors or end users purchase competing products.

2. *Refusal to Deal*: Manufacturers or distributors inform independent suppliers that they will discontinue purchases if the suppliers sell materials to competing businesses.

3. *Market Allocation*: A group of manufacturers or distributors mutually arranges not to deal with each other's customers.

4. *Tied Financing*: A financial firm provides financing for a distributor or end user on the condition that the recipient deals exclusively with a manufacturer who has a relationship with the financial firm.

5. *Obstruction of Distribution*: A manufacturer causes an independent distributor to restrict promotion of a competitor's new product until the manufacturer develops a competitive product.

6. *Retail Price Maintenance*: A manufacturer agrees to repurchase from a retailer unsold inventory at the price paid by the retailer on condition that the retailer maintains the manufacturer's suggested retail price.

7. *Obstruction of Advertising*: A manufacturer threatens to withdraw its advertisements unless advertisements for a competing product are rejected.

8. *Price Fixing*: A group of manufacturers mutually agree to fix the price of a product.

9. *Production Cartel:* A group of manufacturers mutually agree to restrict production and supply of a product.

10. *Bid-Rigging*: Companies bidding for a specific project hold mutual consultations prior to the bidding to determine which company will win the contract.

Respondents were asked to indicate on a five-point scale of "Much Less Often" to "Much More Often" the frequency of occurrence in Japan of the described behavior relative to occurrence in the United States. (The description in italic type face accompanying each of the above scenarios did not appear in the questionnaire. For example, respondents were asked only about the relative frequency of "A group of manufacturers mutually agree to fix the price of a product." The term "price fixing" did not appear in the questionnaire.) The mid-point of the scale indicates that the frequency is the same. Respondents were not asked to judge or comment upon the legality or fairness of the practice, and they were instructed to answer exclusively in reference to markets in which their business unit competes.

As will be reported in Chapter 4, these ten items were analyzed for occurrence and impact on performance both individually and in the aggregate. A principal components factor analysis of the ten behaviors loaded on one factor with high internal consistency (Cronbach alpha = .92) explained 58 percent of the variance (Table 3.9). A summated variable, BEHAVIOR, was constructed for subsequent aggregate analysis.

The Impact of Anticompetitive Behavior

It is possible that foreign business executives may incorrectly perceive anticompetitive behavior to have a negative impact on the performance of their operations in Japan when there may actually be no statistical basis for that perception. In order to check the congruence between the statistical findings and executives' perceptions, respondents were asked to indicate, on a five-point scale ranging from "Strongly Disagree" to "Strongly Agree," if their performance in Japan had been adversely impacted by the occurrence of the anticompetitive behavior described. Principal components factor analysis (Table 3.10) loaded responses to the ten situations on one factor, IMPACT, explaining 64 percent of the total variance with high internal consistency (Cronbach alpha = .94).

Table 3.9
Principal Components Factor Loadings
for the Relative Occurrence of Anticompetitive Behavior

Factors:	Factor 1
Factor Label	BEHAVIOR
Eigenvalue	5.80
Percent of variance	58.0
Cronbach alpha	.92

Variables:	
Refusal to Supply	**.51**
Refusal to Deal	**.63**
Market Allocation	**.73**
Tied Financing	**.58**
Obstruction of Distribution	**.50**
Retail Price Maintenance	.45
Obstruction of Advertising	.45
Price Fixing	**.58**
Production Cartel	**.65**

Table 3.10
Principal Components Factor Loadings
for the Impact of Anticompetitive Behavior

Factors:	Factor 1
Factor Label	IMPACT
Eigenvalue	6.40
Percent of variance	64.0
Cronbach alpha	.94

Variables:	
Refusal to Supply	**.61**
Refusal to Deal	**.69**
Market Allocation	**.70**
Tied Financing	**.75**
Obstruction of Distribution	**.71**
Retail Price Maintenance	**.53**
Obstruction of Advertising	.49
Price Fixing	**.63**
Production Cartel	**.72**
Bid-Rigging	**.58**

(*Note*: Items with factor loadings ≥ 0.5 in **bold** are used to develop a composite measure for subsequent analysis.)

Characteristics of the Market

Based on the literature review, a list of 17 aspects of a market environment were compiled, all of which have been shown in previous studies to have an impact on performance. Respondents were asked to indicate on a five-point scale ranging from "Very Low" to "Very High" the position that best described the conditions of the market in which their business unit operates in Japan. The 17 variables were: (1) market growth rate (1991–1993), (2) expected long-term (1991–2000) market growth rate, (3) average industry gross margins (1991–1993), (4) average industry pretax profits (1991–1993), (5) outlook for future profits (1994–2000), (6) number of competitors, (7) market share concentration of the four largest companies in the market, (8) number of substitute products, (9) number of component suppliers, (10) number of distributors, (11) number of customers, (12) capital investment required to compete in Japan, (13) one-time costs to a buyer due to switching suppliers, (14) cost advantages of Japanese competitors, (15) product differentiation offered by Japanese competitors, (16) intensity of price competition, and (17) extent to which Japan's government limits or controls expansion in the market. After item cleansing and principal components factor analysis with varimax rotation, 14 variables loaded on four factors (Table 3.11). Two of the factors were dropped due to difficulty in interpreting the factor and low internal consistency (Cronbach alpha of .35 and .34 respectively). The remaining two factors explain 39 percent of the variance with good internal consistency, and clean, logical interpretations consistent with the literature that has been reviewed.

The first factor, MARKET, consists of five variables that indicate the growth and profit conditions of the market. The second factor, STRUCTURE, contains five measures of the structure of the market that could serve as barriers to entry or expansion, as postulated by entry theory. For example, if there are few competitors, suppliers, distributors, substitute products, and/or customers, the incumbents may have a greater possibility of creating effective structural barriers to new entrants. Factors 3 and 4 were not considered for further analysis due to their low internal consistency (i.e., Cronbach alpha = .35).

3.11
Varimax Rotated Factor Loadings
for Characteristics of the Market

Factors:	Factor 1	Factor 2	Factor 3	Factor 4
Factor Label	MARKET	STRUCTURE		
Eigenvalue	3.22	2.27	1.93	1.26
Percent of variance	23.0	16.2	13.8	9.0
Cronbach alpha	.74	.78	.35	.34
Variables:				
Market Growth Rate	**.72**	.13	-.06	.07
Long Term Market Growth	**.65**	.17	-.39	.12
Industry Gross Margins	**.72**	-.02	.49	-.20
Industry Pretax Profits	**.77**	-.04	-.42	-.16
Outlook for Future Profits	**.71**	.07	-.05	.25
Number of Competitors	.18	**.76**	.-.15	-.19
Number of Substitutes	-.01	**.69**	-.06	-.11
Number of Suppliers	.04	**.69**	-.25	.06
Number of Distributors	.14	**.76**	.23	-.09
Number of Customers	.04	**.61**	.46	.22
Level of Price Competition	.12	-.17	**.66**	.12
Customer Switching Costs	.12	-.27	**-.74**	.18
Market Share of 4 Largest	-.03	-.10	.18	**.81**
Capital Required in Japan	.17	-.07	-.22	**.66**

(*Note*: Items with factor loadings $\geq$ 0.5 in **bold** are used to develop a composite measure for subsequent analysis.)

Characteristics of the Firm

Twelve dimensions of competitive strength were selected from the literature: (1) product differentiation, (2) breadth of product line, (3) technological innovation, (4) initiating product improvements, (5) competitive pricing, (6) promotional practices, (7) company image, (8) quality of service, (9) service improvements, (10) sales force effectiveness, (11) bargaining position with customers, and (12) economies of scale. Respondents were asked to rate their business unit relative to their competitors in Japan on a five-point scale of "Much Lower" to "Much Better." Item cleansing and principal components factor analysis with varimax rotation resulted in three factors that explain 67 percent of the total variance: SERVICE, PRODUCT, and CLOUT (Table 3.12).

Table 3.12
Varimax Rotated Factor Loadings
for Characteristics of the Firm

Factors:	Factor 1	Factor 2	Factor 3
Factor Label	SERVICE	PRODUCT	CLOUT
Eigenvalue	3.69	1.23	1.07
Percent of variance	41.0	13.7	11.9
Cronbach alpha	.80	.74	.62
Variables:			
Service Quality	**.87**	.20	.14
Service Improvements	**.84**	.25	.12
Sales force Effectiveness	**.70**	.13	.11
Product Differentiation	.25	**.81**	.18
Product Improvement	.31	**.71**	.19
Breadth of Product Line	-.03	**.59**	.50
Technological Innovation	.15	**.70**	-.07
Bargaining Position	.34	.09	**.70**
Economies of Scale	.06	.09	**.87**

(*Note*: Items with factor loadings $\geq$ 0.5 in **bold** are used to develop a composite measure for subsequent analysis.)

SERVICE represents the ability of the firm to provide and continually improve the quality of its service. An effective sales force is important to this factor, as it is generally the sales force that has the closest and most frequent contact with the customer. The sales representative's personal attention to quality can create or detract from a firm's quality image. The PRODUCT factor accounts for competitive advantage that can arise from superior characteristics of the firm's products: a differentiated and wide variety of product offerings, incorporating the latest technology and improvements. The third factor, CLOUT, represents areas of strength through economies of scale and a stronger bargaining position with customers, which could result from many considerations: reputation, technology, experience, size, and so forth.

Strategy

As noted in the literature review, two aspects of a company's strategy are crucial to successful performance in foreign markets: adaptation and autonomy. Of course, this does not imply a complete change of the marketing mix variables for each market, or absolute local control. In many cases only slight modifications are required to what otherwise would be considered a standardized approach. But management must be willing to adapt to local market needs and conditions. In order to meet market demands in a timely and effective manner, management must allow some degree of local autonomy.

To determine the extent to which businesses had adapted their strategies to focus specifically on the needs and demands of customers in Japan, respondents were asked to indicate their agreement, on a five-point scale from "Strongly Disagree" to "Strongly Agree," with the following statements:

- We initiated product changes to better adapt our products to the needs and demands of our Japanese customers.

- We increased our investment in resources dedicated to serving our customers in Japan.

- We heavily promoted our products in Japan.

- It has been our objective to increase our market share in Japan.

- We set aggressive sales goals for our operations in Japan.

Agreement with these statements would indicate that the strategic thrust of a company is to build their business in Japan, rather than to merely maintain or pull back (Burke 1984). It is interesting and encouraging to note that of the 129 companies participating in the survey, 89 percent scored higher than 3.0 on a composite of these measures, which would appear to indicate that the vast majority of U.S. organizations in Japan are attempting to build their operations there.

To measure the degree of local management autonomy, a five-point scale ranging from "Total Control" to "No Control" was used, and executives were asked to indicate the degree of local management control over product, pricing, promotional, and investment decisions for the Japanese market.

A principal components factor analysis with varimax rotation for these nine variables resulted in two factors, AUTONOMY and FOCUS (Table 3.13), explaining 55 percent of the total variance with adequate internal consistency.

Table 3.13
Varimax Rotated Factor Loadings for Strategy

Factors:	Factor 1	Factor 2
Factor Label	AUTONOMY	FOCUS
Eigenvalue	2.80	2.17
Percento of variance	31.1	24.1
Cronbach alpha	.79	.73
Variables:		
Control of Product Mgmt	**.75**	.05
Control of Pricing	**.85**	-.07
Control of Promotion	**.82**	.01
Control of Investment	**.70**	.20
Increase Market Share	-.10	**.66**
Increase Investment	.03	**.70**
Aggressive Sales Goals	.14	**.78**
Heavy Promotion	.17	**.73**
Product Adaption	.01	**.59**

(*Note*: Items with factor loadings $\geq$ 0.5 in **bold** are used to develop a composite measure for subsequent analysis.)

Performance

Common measures of performance are market share and profitability (e.g., Burke 1984, Buzzell and Gale 1987, Day and Wensley 1988, Doyle, Saunders, and Wong 1992, Kotabe 1990). Using a five-point scale of "Much Lower" to "Much Higher," executives were asked to assess the performance of their business unit on three criteria, relative to their three largest competitors in Japan: (1) market share, (2) pretax profits, and (3) return on investment. A principal components factor analysis (Table 3.14) supports the computation of one factor, PERFORM, to represent the construct of recent performance. The single factor explains 63 percent of the variance and has reasonable internal consistency (Cronbach alpha = .69).

In a recent presentation at the University of Texas, C. K. Prahalad introduced the concept of "opportunity share." According to this idea, in some cases it may be more appropriate to measure performance by how well one captures future opportunities rather than judging by current or past profits and market share. Opportu-

Table 3.14
Principal Components Factor Loadings
for Recent Three-Year Performance

Factors:	Factor 1
Factor Label	PERFORM
Eigenvalue	1.88
Percent of variance	62.6
Cronbach alpha	.69
Variables:	
Market Share	**.56**
Pretax Profits	**.89**
Return on Investment	**.88**

(*Note*: Items with factor loadings $\geq$ 0.5 in **bold** are used to develop a composite measure for subsequent analysis.)

nity share seems an appropriate measure in this situation considering that many of the U.S. businesses doing business in Japan currently have a very small share of the market. Yet, as noted earlier, the vast majority are building their operations in Japan. Therefore, in an attempt to capture this construct, executives were also asked to evaluate their likelihood of improvement during the next three years on the same three dimensions (market share, pretax profits, and return on investment), relative to their three largest competitors. A principal components factor analysis (Table 3.15) loads the three variables well on one factor (PROSPECT), explaining 67 percent of the variance, and with high internal consistency (Cronbach alpha = .73).

Factors Not Considered in the Model

As noted earlier, the views of Japanese and American executives regarding the relative frequency of anticompetitive activity in Japan vary considerably. Differences in nationality could likewise have some bearing on the operation of the model. Thus, the nationality of the respondent (American, Japanese, Other) is introduced into the model as the control variable NATION.

A company's experience in a market could also be an important influence on performance, although the competitive advantage provided by experience would most likely diminish over time as

Table 3.15
Principal Components Factor Loadings
for Expected Three-Year Performance

Factors:	Factor 1
Factor Label	PROSPECT
Eigenvalue	1.99
Percent of variance	66.5
Cronbach alpha	.73
Variables:	
Market Share	**.62**
Pretax Profits	**.91**
Return on Investment	**.88**

(Note: Items with factor loadings ≥ 0.5 in **bold** used to develop a composite measure for subsequent analysis.)

other businesses became equally seasoned participants. Several researchers have found a positive correlation between international business experience (and the knowledge that experience brings) and better performance (Fenwick and Amine 1979, Glejser, Jacquemin, and Petit 1980). The control variable EXPERT was calculated for each responding company based on a five-point scale consistent with the experience intervals shown in Table 3.8.

4

Analyses and Results

OCCURRENCE OF ANTICOMPETITIVE BEHAVIOR

It was hypothesized that anticompetitive behavior occurs more frequently in Japan than in the United States. As explained earlier, to test this hypothesis, business executives in Japan were given descriptions of ten types of behavior and asked to indicate the rate of occurrence in Japan relative to the United States using a five-point scale on which the midpoint implied no difference in the relative rate of activity. Thus, a mean score significantly different from 3.00 would denote a rate of occurrence in Japan distinct from practices in the United States. Mean scores were computed for each of the ten types of anticompetitive behavior individually and in the aggregate as the factor BEHAVIOR. These were tested for significant difference ($p < .05$) from a hypothetical mean of 3.00. The results are shown in Table 4.1.

The analysis indicates that anticompetitive behavior does occur more frequently in Japan then in the United States, supporting the hypothesis. This is true in both the aggregate (BEHAVIOR) and individually for six of the ten types of anticompetitive behavior investigated: bid-rigging, price fixing, market allocation,

Table 4.1

Relative Occurrence of Anticompetitive Behavior in Japan

Anticompetitive Behavior	All		Americans		Japanese		Other	
	Mean	Std. Dev.	Mean	Std. Dev.	Mean	Std. Dev.	Mean	Std. Dev.
Bid Rigging	**3.54**	0.95	**3.87**	0.87	3.11	0.91	**3.67**	0.87
Price Fixing	**3.53**	1.00	**3.80**	0.87	3.13	1.07	**3.73**	0.90
Market Allocation	**3.43**	0.96	**3.68**	0.97	3.13	0.89	3.43	0.85
Tied Financing	**3.39**	0.91	**3.51**	0.82	3.21	1.02	**3.50**	0.76
Production Cartel	**3.27**	1.11	**3.46**	0.66	3.02	0.94	3.30	0.95
Refusal to Supply	**3.22**	1.02	**3.57**	0.97	2.77	1.17	3.21	0.89
Retail Price Maintenance	3.16	0.78	**3.48**	0.95	2.80	0.99	3.17	1.03
Obstruction of Distribution	3.13	0.89	**3.33**	0.70	2.86	0.85	3.21	0.70
Refusal to Deal	3.08	0.83	**3.32**	0.79	2.83	0.90	2.92	1.04
Obstruction of Advertising	2.90	0.73	**3.22**	0.69	**2.51**	0.83	3.00	0.85
BEHAVIOR (see Table 3.9) (Cronbach alpha = .92)	**3.21**	0.73	**3.52**	0.63	2.88	0.67	3.28	0.82

(*Note*: Scores in **bold** typeface indicate a significant difference (p < . 05) from a mean of 3.00.)

tied financing, production cartels, and refusal to supply. These findings should be interpreted with caution, however, because, as noted earlier, an analysis of variance by nationality of executive showed substantial differences in their perceptions of anticompetitive activity. When mean scores are calculated according to the respondent's nationality, the results are striking. American executives felt that all ten types of behavior occur more frequently in Japan than the United States, while Japanese executives felt that none of the activities happens more often in Japan. Executives of other nationalities (e.g., Canadian, Australian, European) fell between these two extremes, indicating that they believe bid-rigging, price fixing and tied financing are more common in Japan than in the United States.

It is surprising that the American and Japanese executives hold such opposite views regarding the occurrence of anticompetitive behavior, especially considering that the executives are all employed as senior officers with U.S. companies. Of course, differences in culture and experience can lead to divergent perceptions and interpretations of identical activities. Such phenomena are the basis for the emic versus etic dilemma within international research. The emic school of thought asserts that attitudinal and behavioral phenomena are unique to a culture, while the etic side searches for universal attitudinal and behavioral measures. The researchers had initially thought it would be possible to avoid culture-specific complications by polling executives of U.S. companies exclusively. In addition, the respondents were given identical descriptions of various behaviors and were asked to indicate only the relative frequency of the behavior, not its legality, so as to make it unlikely that the responses would vary by nationality due to differences in interpretation of, or experience with, fair trade laws. For example, it was assumed that executives could disagree about whether bid-rigging is a violation of antitrust laws without hampering their ability to judge relative frequency of occurrence. But this does not appear to be the case. Clearly the American executives see what they judge to be anticompetitive behavior occurring more frequently in Japan than do the Japanese businessmen.

Furthermore, the Japanese executives' perception that the relative occurrence of the anticompetitive behaviors described was relatively similar in both the United States and Japan is not necessarily without basis, either. As reported in Episode 2.1 in Chapter 2, in an interview regarding Kodak's complaint to the U.S. Trade Representative under Section 301, the senior managing director of Fuji Photo Film, Masayuki Muneyuki, told the Nikkei Weekly that the United States market is as difficult to access as Japan's. When asked what barriers Fuji had encountered in the U.S., Mr. Muneyuki said, "Apart from the 3.7 percent tariff in the U.S., which Japan does not have, there is nothing I would call a barrier—just as there is none in Japan. But there are tremendous marketing efforts to defend the home market, which sometimes makes us wonder if it might not be in violation of antitrust law. Some, such as highly progressive rebates, would certainly be illegal under Japan's Antimonopoly Law. U.S. antitrust law has strict aspects, but it also has lenient aspects, as in allowing highly progressive rebates. Its strict points are often emphasized as if to say Japanese law is too soft. Japanese regulations are quite strict on influencing prices" ("Fuji Photo to Kodak: Stand on Your Own," *Nikkei Weekly*, October 23, 1995).

Given the long and proactive history of antitrust enforcement in the United States and the contrary situation in Japan, it is also conceivable that what an American executive may interpret to be an anticompetitive act is considered by Japanese business executives to be normal business behavior. Americans may attribute anticompetitive intentions where none were intended. President Clinton recently advised Boris Yeltsin that when the Japanese say "yes" they really mean "no."[1] If diplomats at that level have difficulty interpreting the meaning of Japanese words and actions, perhaps American executives, conditioned by the enforcement practices in their own country, may suppose more sinister implications within observed behavior than was intended. On the other hand, the Japanese executives may have felt it inappropriate to surmise anticompetitive implications to more subtle forms of communication that did not directly and obviously match the behavior described in the questionnaire.

Another possible, but less likely, explanation for the different points of view could be that the Japanese respondents may not be sufficiently familiar with the competitive climate in the United States. They may have had little question about the anticompetitive nature of the acts described, but could believe that the behavior is more common in the United States than is actually the case. However, over two-thirds of the Japanese respondents have been with their American employer for more than five years, which should imply some familiarity with American business practices. They had undoubtedly participated in business meetings with American executives during which various strategies and business practices of the company and its competitors were reviewed. And their employers would have been rather reckless if they had not informed their Japanese officers about United States antitrust rules and their extraterritorial application to the company. Nevertheless, these experiences alone might not have created an understanding comparable to that held by U.S. executives of the severity of the enforcement climate in the U.S. and the strict interpretations applied to various behaviors.

Nationalistic pride is a possible, but also less probable, explanation for the differences in the executives' evaluations. Although the behaviors were not described as anticompetitive or unfair, and the executives were not asked to evaluate their legality, the nature of the activities described would be rather obvious to any seasoned business executive. An American executive, frustrated by an inability to succeed in Japan, could overstate the occurrence of anticompetitive behavior. Likewise, Japanese executives, wanting to protect Japan's reputation and honor, could understate the level of activity. This possibility seems unlikely, however, because it is not consistent with the responses to the balance of the questionnaire. No other critical response patterns varied by nationality, particularly the assessment of the impact of anticompetitive behavior, which will be reviewed later in this chapter.

In conclusion, the first hypothesis is answered affirmatively by U.S. executives working in Japan but rejected by their Japanese colleagues. American executives clearly believe they face more anticompetitive behavior in Japan than they do in the United States. In particular, bid-rigging, price fixing, market allocation, tied financing, production cartels, and refusal to supply are areas of greater perceived anticompetitive activity. Yet Japanese executives of U.S. companies do not agree that anticompetitive behavior occurs more frequently in Japan. Executives of other nationalities fall between these two divergent opinions.

As illustrated in Episode 4.1, the recorded music industry in Japan offers a typical case example in which the executives of different nationalities may interpret the same situation quite differently. This is a case of legal price maintenance, which may give foreigners a false impression of illegal price fixing. Further, considering that some of the record companies in Japan are subsidiaries and/or affiliates of U.S. companies, this may be a good example of why foreign companies that have established themselves within the existing business climate in Japan may not be in a hurry to see it changed. This point is elaborated upon in the next section.

Episode 4.1
Confusion and Interpretational Differences—Records,
Tapes, and Compact Discs

Japanese record companies have not faced all-out competition on the price front for more than 40 years. Manufacturer price fixing is generally prohibited by the nation's Antimonopoly Law, but makers of recorded music, books, medicines, and cosmetics have been allowed to require that retailers sign no-discount contracts or retail price maintenance contracts. The law grants manufacturers of these items the authority to unilaterally set the retail prices of their products. Government officials said they originally drafted the exemption into the Antimonopoly Law to prevent excessive price-cutting competition that could threaten the quality of the goods. But in 1991, with rising pressure from consumers unhappy about paying some of the highest prices in the world for their CDs and tapes, Japan's Fair Trade Commission began to reevaluate the music exemption.

Noboru Takayama, chairman of the Japan Phonograph Record Association (JPRA), believes there are special circumstances which warrant the continuation of retail price controls. "Because we use a resale system, our products can be sold under the same conditions anywhere in the country, and composers can continue writing even when sales are relatively small," he said. "There is a far wider range of records available in Japan than overseas. New U.S. releases number only half as many as in Japan, while production efficiency there is high since on average six times as many copies of each new release are pressed. In addition, costs are lower since masters can be sold to other countries, especially English speaking ones. By contrast, Japanese companies are dependent on the domestic market."

Tsutomu Ueno, manager of international sales and marketing at Nippon Columbia Corp., one of the leading CD manufacturers in Japan, echoes Takayama's opinion. He believes that the low profile of Japanese pop musicians abroad makes manufacturers heavily reliant on the local market for profits. "Our export volume accounts for no more than 10 percent of total production. On the other hand, U.S. manufacturers are able to lower their prices because they can sell CDs throughout the world," he said.

"Ninety percent of the record shops in Japan are mom-and-pop stores which would not be able to make a profit if free competition is introduced because they do not have enough floor space to boost sales and compensate for a reduced profit margin," adds Fumio Iwata, director of the Japan Record Retailers Association.

The JFTC finally recommended a partial lifting of the price controls, which JPRA "voluntarily" adopted, allowing retail shops to discount recorded music products that are either imported or more than two years old. The manufacturers could continue to set the retail price of domestically produced CDs and tapes during the first two years following their release.

Sankyo Shoji Trading Co. found that they could purchase Japanese CDs in other Asian countries for ¥300–400 less than the wholesale price in Japan. They could then "import" the CDs and legally sell them at a discount. For example, a CD featuring Japan's popular duo, Chage and Aska, sells for ¥3,200 at ordinary stores compared with ¥2,480 at stores that deal with Sankyo Shoji.

"If the manufacturers are able to sell CDs overseas at those prices, why can't they do the same in Japan?" asks Hiroshi Takeuchi, president of Sankyo Shoji Trading Co. "The CD makers have been making too much profit and the high price tags on CDs have prevented the music culture in Japan from spreading to age groups such as the elderly and children who have less income."

Sources: "Retain Uniform Pricing for CDs, Tapes: Industry Head," *Nikkei Weekly*, August 31, 1991; "CD Reimporter Cracks Cartel Pricing System," *Nikkei Weekly*, May 16, 1992; and "New Music Pricing Scheme Cuts CD Prices from Nov. 1," *Daily Yomiuri*, Thursday, October 29, 1992.

IMPACT OF ANTICOMPETITIVE BEHAVIOR

The second hypothesis concerns the impact of anticompetitive behavior on the performance of U.S. companies marketing manufactured products in Japan. An analysis of covariance was performed using recent three year performance and the prospect for expected three-year performance as the dependent variables (PERFORM and PROSPECT, respectively). Independent variables included factors for growth and profit conditions (MARKET), market structure (STRUCTURE), competitive strengths in service (SERVICE), product offerings (PRODUCT), economies of scale and bargaining position (CLOUT), local management control (AUTONOMY), and adaptation to the Japanese market (FOCUS). The factor BEHAVIOR, aggregating the ten anticompetitive activities, was also an independent variable. (Analyses performed using each individual type of anticompetitive behavior as an independent variable produced nearly identical results, so only the aggregate results will be reported.) The company's years of experience in Japan (EXPERT) and the nationality of the respondent (NATION) were input as control variables. The model had good explanatory power (R^2 = 40% and 32% respectively). The results are shown in Table 4.2.

Contrary to the hypothesis, anticompetitive behavior (BEHAVIOR) has not had a significant impact on the recent performance

Table 4.2
Analysis of Covariance (ANCOVA) of Factors Influencing Recent Three-Year Performance (PERFORM) and Expected Three-Year Performance (PROSPECT) of U.S. Businesses in Japan

	PERFORM		PROSEPCT	
Factor	*Coefficient Estimate*	*t-value*	*Coefficient Estimate*	*t-value*
Intercept	-.85	-	1.49	-
BEHAVIOR	-.13	100	-.14c	-1.35
MARKET	-.13	-.1.07	-.21b	-.2.14
STRUCTURE	.18b	1.70	.26a	3.04
SERVICE	.25b	2.12	.06	0.60
PRODUCT	.18c	1.44	.14c	1.40
CLOUT	.31a	3.07	18b	2.28
AUTONOMY	.11	1.19	.16b	2.09
FOCUS	.00	0.03	.20b	1.95
EXPERT*	.14a	2.72	-.02	-0.57
NATION				
Japanese*	.30	1.61	.09	0.62
Other*	-.13	-0.52	-.56a	-2.71
American	-	-	-	-
R^2	40.1%		32.0%	-

[a]$p = <.01$
[b]$p = <.05$
[c]$p = <.10$

*two-tailed t-tests; all other variables are one-tailed t-tests.

of U.S. companies in Japan. The most significant factors in determining performance were experience (EXPERT) and the company's strengths derived from economies of scale and advantageous bargaining position (CLOUT). The influence of market structure was as expected, with greater numbers of competitors, distributors, and suppliers (STRUCTURE) facilitating ease of entry and better performance. Not surprisingly, other competitive strengths derived from superior service (SERVICE) and the product attributes (PRODUCT) also proved important to recent performance.

When these executives look ahead at performance in the coming years, a somewhat different set of variables becomes important. Anticompetitive behavior (BEHAVIOR) does begin to have an effect, although it is only a marginally significant factor ($p < .10$). Executives apparently feel that they have been able to successfully penetrate the Japanese market and achieve their corporate perform- ance objectives despite the occurrence of such activities. However, as they look ahead and consider further growth and expansion (their "opportunity share"), they appear to be concerned that anticompetitive practices could inhibit their performance. Consid- ering the situation of many U.S. companies in Japan, this is not an unreasonable evaluation. In many industries, U.S. companies have the highest market share of any foreign competitors and they earn very good profits on their Japan sales. However, those market shares are relatively small when compared with their domestic competitors. The executives may be concerned that as they attempt to gain an even larger share of the market, the anticompetitive behavior of domestic firms could inhibit their expansion plans. The movie industry (Episode 4.2) is a good example of an industry in which U.S. companies have done extremely well despite some barriers, but still have vast potential if they can overcome those barriers.

Episode 4.2
A Great Success or Just Scratching the Surface?—Hollywood in Japan

Some U.S. companies are doing well despite Japanese anticompe- titive business practices. For example, Japan has become the biggest foreign market for U.S. movies. In 1990 the U.S. majors took in $236 million from film rentals in Japan. But Time Warner and other Western film companies feel they could do much better. It is not easy for foreign filmmakers to get their product into the relatively small number of theaters that exist in Japan (one movie screen for every 60,000 Japanese versus, one for every 10,000 Americans). Two Japanese cinema companies control the release of most foreign films in Japan. One is $1.2 billion Toho Co., known in the West for its Godzilla movies. The other is $400 million Shochiku Co., Japan's oldest film producer. Toho and Shochiku exert nearly total control over the release of all foreign movies in Japan, and over the majority of Japanese films as well. Thanks to Japan's weak antitrust laws, they are able to reserve theaters nationwide for Japanese movies and fix the length of the runs of their own movies, even if they are unpopular. If independently owned theaters in the major markets want access to the first-run foreign movies or films produced or distributed by Toho or Shochiku, they must agree to run everything the companies pick. It is similar to the kind of block booking outlawed in the United States decades ago. But in Japan antitrust laws are weak and rarely enforced.

So U.S. distributors cannot afford to offend these quasi-monopoly companies. Says Jean-Louis Rubin, at one time head of Twentieth Century Fox's international division and more recently with Largo Entertainment, "If you get into a fight with one company, then you are stuck with the other." U.S. studios can show their productions through Toho-affiliated theaters or Shochiku-affiliated theaters, but never both. Thus, even a wildly popular foreign film will open at a maximum of 8 theaters in Tokyo (population 12 million).

What if a foreign film company were to deal directly with an urban independent Japanese theater owner? Toho officials say they would not retaliate against a company that did that. Believe that if you will. Says the head of one big foreign distributor, "We would like to deal with exhibitors directly, but we cannot because Toho might stop dealing with us or we might be stuck in second-run theaters."

Toho and Shochiku make no apologies for their tactics. They complain that the foreign distributors in Japan are too strong already.

Source: Adapted from Gale Eisenstodt, "A Cozy Japanese Near Monopoly," *Forbes*, September 30, 1991.

Product strengths (PRODUCT), bargaining position, and economies of scale (CLOUT) continue to be consequential variables enhancing future performance, with local management autonomy (AUTONOMY) and the adaptation of marketing mix variables to local needs, tastes and competitive practices (FOCUS) increasing in importance. This is not surprising, as these are factors that research consistently shows to be essential for successful international market expansion. For example, Czinkota and Kotabe (1993) asked business executives, policy makers, and researchers how foreign companies could improve their ability to penetrate the Japanese market. Market research, product adaptation, collaborative ventures and overall better business strategy were seen as more beneficial than trade negotiations.

SERVICE loses some of its significance when looking toward future performance. This may at first seem surprising, until one considers the well-deserved reputation of Japanese companies for service. It may be that U.S. companies find it necessary to place great emphasis on service when entering a market and winning new customers. Over the long term, however, once parity is reached with domestic Japanese suppliers on service quality, it may be more difficult to gain a competitive advantage in this area.

Experience (EXPERT) has diminishing value over time, as expected. Market conditions (MARKET), that is, growth rates and profit margins, have a substantial impact on opportunity share, but in the opposite direction of what was anticipated, perhaps for fear that high growth and fat margins will attract increased competition. Another unexpected outcome is the significant negative coefficient for executives of non-Japanese, non-American nationality. These foreign business leaders apparently have lower expectations for future performance than their American counterparts. One possibility for this finding may be their unbiased and more pessimistic view of the direction U.S.–Japan relations are headed. Another cause could be their greater familiarity with the economic situation in Europe and some attribution of future negative consequences for all international trade.

It is interesting to note that the ANCOVA results regarding the impact of anticompetitive behavior on recent performance are consistent with executives' perceptions. Concurrent with their evaluation of the relative frequency of the ten anticompetitive practices, executives were also asked to assess the impact of each activity on their business. Using a five-point scale, only mean scores significantly greater than 3.00 would indicate a negative influence on performance. As shown in Table 4.3, there is no single case, within the total group of respondents or by nationality, where it can be said conclusively that a particular behavior affects performance. On the other hand, it can be said conclusively ($p < .05$) that these executives believe that price fixing, obstruction of distribution, retail price maintenance, production cartels, and obstruction of advertising do not adversely affect U.S. business performance in Japan. So although the American and Japanese executives disagreed about the rate of occurrence, they do agree

Table 4.3

The Impact of Anticompetitive Behavior in Japan on U.S. Businesses

Anticompetitive Behavior	*All*		*Americans*		*Japanese*		*Other*	
	Mean	*Std. Dev.*	*Mean*	*Std. Dev.*	*Mean*	*Std. Dev.*	*Mean*	*Std. Dev.*
Refusal to Supply	2.93	1.32	2.95	1.38	3.12	1.32	2.71	1.07
Bid-Rigging	2.99	1.29	2.95	1.41	2.91	1.20	2.90	1.10
Refusal to Deal	2.82	1.17	2.76	1.13	2.98	1.28	2.54	0.97
Market Allocation	2,82	1.17	2.92	1.29	2.79	1.07	**2.50**	0.85
Tied Financing	2.82	1.20	2.69	1.18	2.98	1.28	2.79	0.97
Price Fixing	**2.75**	1.18	2.74	1.21	2.80	1.19	2.58	1.08
Obstruction of Distribution	**2.66**	1.23	**2.51**	1.27	2.86	1.25	2.64	0.93
Retail Price Maintenance	**2.60**	1.18	**2.49**	1.10	2.68	1.25	2.69	1.25
Production Cartel	**2.59**	1.14	**2.55**	1.10	2.72	1.23	**2.27**	1.01
Obstruction of Advertising	**2.39**	1.11	**2.31**	1.10	**2.45**	1.15	2.46	1.05

(*Note*: Scores in **bold** typeface indicate a significant difference ($p < .05$) from a mean of 3.00.)

that anticompetitive behavior has not had a negative impact on their results.

In summary, the second hypothesis is not supported. The occurrence of anticompetitive behavior has not had a negative impact on the recent business performance of U.S. companies marketing manufactured goods in Japan. This must be qualified, however, because U.S. business executives do expect that such behavior could become an impediment as they expand their presence in Japan.

Given the wide variety of U.S. industries participating in this study (24 general categories), and the relatively few number of respondents within each industry, it is difficult to reach any definitive conclusions regarding anticompetitive behavior on an industry-by-industry basis. In some industries, well-established foreign companies may actually benefit from established Japanese practices (See Episode 4.3).

Episode 4.3
Some Practices Benefit Foreign Firms, Too—The Satellite Industry

Since Tokyo opened the market to international bidders in April 1990, all three commercial satellites bought by Japan—worth as much as $200 million each—were sold by American companies. Although Washington is again threatening to retaliate against Japan for closed markets in eight industries, it appears to have no complaints with the Japanese commercial satellite market. Yet while the Super 301 action may have succeeded in opening Japan's commercial satellite market, it has left a bitter taste on both sides of the Pacific. Japanese manufacturers feel slighted, yet remain determined to compete with the United States in the $15–billion-a-year business of building commercial satellites. American satellite companies, which once made big margins selling subsystems to the Japanese, have become prime contractors and increased their total sales in Japan. But cutthroat competition has trimmed profits to nearly nothing. And there has been little, if any, impact from the agreement on the gaping trade imbalance between Japan and the United States. Satellites sold by American companies are shipped not to Japan, but to launch sites in the United States or elsewhere.

Many would be pleased to return to the old system of cozy government-industry ties and fat margins. "Before, everybody made good money," said Arlo Brown, vice-president of Martin Marietta International in Japan. "But ever since the Japanese began making very fair satellite procurements, the American competitors have been tearing each others' hair out."

Source: Adapted from Steven Brull, "Japan Satellite Market's Opening to U.S. is a Dud for Both Sides," *International Herald Tribune*, March 12, 1994.

In other industries, anticompetitive practices do appear to have a negative effect. A simple calculation, excluding industries with fewer than three respondents, and choosing only those industries in which a majority of the respondents indicated both a greater occurrence of a specific behavior *and* a negative impact on business performance, suggests that anticompetitive activity varies notably depending upon the industry. As shown in Table 4.4, seven industries apparently face more damaging anticompetitive obstacles. In general, these industries are centered around industrial rather than

Table 4.4

Industries in Which the Majority of Responding Executives Perceive Both the Occurrence of Anticompetitive Behavior and a Negative Impact on Performance

Industry	Anticompetitive Behavior
Aerospace	Bid-Rigging, Price Fixing
Autos & Auto Parts	Market Allocation, Refusal to Supply
Chemicals	Price Fixing, Tied Financing
Computers	Bid-Rigging
Metals & Metal Products	Refusal to Deal, Refusal to Supply
Publishing	Price Fixing
Paper	Market Allocation, Price Fixing, Refusal to Supply

consumer goods, and appear to be industries in which more traditional vertical keiretsu are strong. However, further research on an industry-by-industry basis will be needed to reach valid conclusions.

NOTE

1. In reality, this flipflop of "yes" and "no" is more accidental than intentional, and is attributed to the way the Japanese speak Japanese. To a negative question, "Don't you agree with me?," a Japanese may say "No" to mean "Yes." He/She meant to say in a typical Japanese grammatical structure, "*No*, it is *not* true that I don't agree with you" (which means "Yes, I agree with you").

Conclusions, Implications, and Recommendations

The findings of this research are both clear and surprising: American business executives working and residing in Japan believe that anticompetitive behavior occurs more frequently in Japan than it does in the United States. Japanese executives of U.S. operations in Japan do not agree, claiming that there is very little difference in the anticompetitive climates of the two countries. What is surprising is that despite their contrary opinions regarding occurrence, the executives agree that anticompetitive behavior has not had a negative influence on their business performance in Japan, although they foresee the potential for adverse consequences upon their future performance. These findings have important implications for U.S. and Japanese businesses, Japanese companies, U.S. and Japanese trade officials, and Japan's Fair Trade Commission.

IMPLICATIONS FOR BUSINESS OPERATIONS

It is troubling that even among the executives of U.S. companies in Japan, the American and Japanese managers appear to interpret competitive behavior quite differently. If the executives of American companies cannot agree, it is not surprising that the leaders of

Japan's corporations express puzzlement when accusations of anticompetitive behavior are raised by the United States. Clearly, additional educational efforts are called for toward helping business people of each nationality understand how various types of behavior are perceived, interpreted, and countered.

American executives must better understand what types of competitive behavior are allowed under Japan's Antimonopoly Law and normal business practices, and how the extraterritorial reach of U.S. antitrust law covers their operations in Japan. Due to erroneous assumptions of illegality, U.S. businesses may be disadvantaged to the extent that they refrain from practices engaged in by their Japanese competitors that are in fact legal in Japan. Japanese business executives must better understand what types of behavior their American trading partners consider to be anticompetitive and take steps to either explain why such practices are allowed in Japan, or, if the activity is in fact a violation of Japan's antitrust laws, eradicate the practice.

Japan's Fair Trade Commission has recently undertaken greater efforts to educate Japanese businesses about what constitutes anticompetitive behavior under Japanese law. In addition to these efforts, organizations such as the U.S.–Japan Business Council, the American Chamber of Commerce, Keidanren, and the Japanese Chamber of Commerce and Industry could work together to sponsor opportunities for joint education of American and Japanese executives. Dialogue must be increased to improve mutual understanding of what is acceptable competitive behavior and what is not.

Although it is a logical assumption that anticompetitive behavior would have a negative influence on business performance, the respondents in this study have indicated otherwise. This finding is consistent with prior research in which nonexporters have been found to perceive export barriers as more formidable obstacles than is actually the case for those who are exporting (Kedia and Chokar 1986). A company that perceives an anticompetitive threat may abort plans to enter a market without sufficiently testing the accuracy of those perceptions. The findings of this study should encourage businesses interested in establishing operations in Japan and keep them from prematurely abandoning strategies due to perceived obstacles. One such example of a company that has pursued the Japanese market despite substantial barriers is the American shoe company, Dexter, as illustrated in Episode 5.1.

Episode 5.1
Overcoming Barriers—Dexter's Shoe Sales in Japan

When U.S. cobblers got trampled by a wave of foreign-made footwear in the 1970s, a modest, family-run shoemaker based in Dexter, Maine, rationalized its operations and emerged as one of the few survivors. Now, Dexter Shoe Co. is trying to sell shoes in Japan.

The marketing problem that Dexter's distributor is facing in Japan is the Japanese government's quota on the number of imported shoes it can sell at the standard 27 percent tariff rate: 7,312 pairs every six months. Above this quota the Japanese government imposes a punitive tariff of 60 percent, making retail prices prohibitively high. And a catch-22 prevents importers from expanding their quotas, which, in principle, are allocated on the basis of the number of shoes already being imported. In other words, a shoe distributor had to sell foreign shoes last year to import them again this year.

Japan's protected shoe industry offers one of the most blatant examples of the kind of market barriers frequently criticized by U.S. exporters. At the heart of the shoe barrier is a delicate political and murky social taboo in the Japanese leather and footwear industry allegedly dominated by the "*burakumin*," a hereditary caste discriminated against over the ages for engaging in "unclean" trades such as tanning and mortuary work. To compensate for past and present injustices, the government shields the leather industry from foreign competition.

Despite the difficulties in Japan, Dexter has been making sincere efforts to crack into the Japanese market. After being approached by Pyle and a Japanese distributor in 1986, the company retooled, investing $200,000 in new equipment to make shoes sized for Japanese feet, in the hope that it could export 50,000 pairs worth about $1.5 million a year. In 1987, Dexter shipped 35,000 pairs of shoes after its Japanese distributor acquired options on unused import quotas from other dealers, but in 1988 the quota was suddenly cut in half, resulting in an inflated inventory of unsold shoes customized for the Japanese market.

In the meantime, Dexter is constantly being shopped by the big Japanese trading houses that broker in the coveted shoe import quotas.

While Dexter could do more business in Japan if it went with one of the large trading companies, the company has remained loyal to the family-run distributor, Chukyo Moonstar of Nagoya, which has been conscientiously promoting Dexter's image in Japan as well as lobbying for an increased quota to sell the shoes. Trust, loyalty, and long-term commitment may eventually work in Dexter's favor.

Source: Adapted from Karl Schoenberger, "U.S. Firm Finds if Shoe Fits, Japan Still May Not Buy It," *Daily Yomiuri*, June 1, 1990.

As has been shown time and time again, the key to successful entry into Japan remains a good business strategy centered around quality products and services that have been adapted to the local market through careful market research (e.g., Czinkota and Kotabe 1993). The results summarized earlier in Table 4.2 reaffirm that foreign companies with the best performance in Japan are those that offer superior products and exceptional service backed by a competitive advantage such as greater economies of scale or another source of bargaining strength. Direct experience and participation in the market is vital, although the contribution toward performance diminishes over time. The long-term growth and performance of U.S. companies in Japan also depends on their developing sufficient local autonomy and flexibility to facilitate timely adaptation to local needs and demands.

Business executives indicated a concern that as they expand their operations in Japan, anticompetitive behavior could become a deterrent. Further research toward an understanding of how businesses have thus far avoided negative consequences of anticompetitive acts would be particularly useful to these executives. Such barriers can be overcome, and foreign companies need a better understanding of the means whereby this is accomplished. These executives can also continue to pressure Japanese business organizations (e.g., Keidanren), consumer organizations, the Japanese government, and their respective governments to work together for the control and elimination of anticompetitive behavior.

IMPLICATIONS FOR TRADE OFFICIALS

Krugman (1994) has recently argued that national living standards are overwhelmingly determined by domestic factors rather than by competition for world markets. Lincoln (1990), Bergsten and Noland (1993) and others claim that the complete removal of alleged trade barriers would not eliminate Japan's surplus with the United States, although it could have a noticeable impact. Haley (1990) and Richards (1993) both argue that better antitrust enforcement in Japan will not improve the trade imbalance. Ryans (1988) found that while nontariff barriers did influence success in Japan, they were a less important factor than some of the more traditional marketing variables. Considering these various points, combined with the findings of this study, it is likely that trade negotiators and business executives who insist on aggressive antitrust enforcement in Japan in anticipation of more open markets, greater sales, and more balanced trade will be disappointed.

On the other hand, to the extent that anticompetitive behavior actually does occur in Japan, these observations do not diminish the pertinence of calls for the removal of such barriers and for more effective AML enforcement. A stronger and more effective enforcement regime will help improve Japan's image as a fair trading partner, a development which would have benefits for Japan, the United States, and the world economy.

Lincoln (1990) points out that "even if American perceptions are exaggerated and one-sided, the sense that Japan gains at American expense in the current trade system will further erode support for the system" (p. 5). The perception of unfair Japanese trading practices is a key element in explaining why U.S. congressional support for liberal trade has declined. "Regardless of whether such beliefs are accurate, the important thing is that they exist. The perception that Japan cheats in the marketplace damages not only Japan's long-term credibility and standing abroad but also the fabric of a free trade system upon which Japan so heavily depends" (Toyama, Tateishi, and Palenberg 1983, p. 609). It is in Japan's own interest, more than those of any of Japan's trading partners, to take steps to improve Japan's fair trade image. Adequately enforcing the AML could contribute considerably to such a change. It is recommended that trade officials from both the United States and Japan continue to pursue the goals set out in the Structural Impediments Initiative relative to strengthening Japan's Fair Trade Commission and more effectively enforcing Japan's Antimonopoly Law.

U.S. trade officials may also find it useful to undertake better education of government policy makers and American business firms regarding the nature of Japanese competitive practices and what different approaches might improve the probability of success in Japan. Concurrently, the U.S. must help American executives understand the extraterritorial application of U.S. antitrust laws to their Japan operations, specifically in reference to areas where U.S. and Japanese laws and practices may vary.

IMPLICATIONS FOR JAPAN'S FAIR TRADE COMMISSION

The evidence of this study suggests that U.S. business executives in Japan do not consider current enforcement of Japan's Antimonopoly Law to be sufficient. In several quotations cited earlier in this work, opinions were expressed that the AML was imposed upon Japan by the U.S. occupation forces, that it is alien to Japanese culture and practice, and that the law cannot be fully enforced because it lacks popular support. The legitimacy of these claims is questionable, but the argument seems moot for at least two reasons. First, the occupation ended over 40 years ago, during which time the Diet first weakened, then strengthened the AML. The premise that the law was forced upon Japan is shaky (First 1993), but in the ensuing decades there has been ample opportunity to debate and adapt the law to Japan's particular needs.

Second, Japan's participation in the world economy requires some conformity to international business practices and rules. It is unrealistic to expect Japanese companies to enjoy the protection afforded by antitrust laws in foreign markets without extending similar protection to foreign companies conducting business in Japan. Japan's antitrust practices need not be the same as those of the United States, and in fact are considered more similar to those of Germany (Haley 1984), but the law and its enforcement must meet a minimum international standard of acceptance.

It is the sole responsibility of Japan's Fair Trade Commission to enforce Japan's Antimonopoly Law; no other domestic or foreign organization has the necessary authority. If evidence exists that potential violations of the AML are occurring, it is incumbent upon the JFTC to investigate and take action to either eliminate the anticompetitive activity or educate the business community as to why the behavior is not illegal. The *Guidelines* recently issued by the JFTC declare that the activities described and investigated in this study are violations *in principle* of the AML. The U.S. executives surveyed indicated that they believe these anticompetitive behaviors (in particular bid-rigging, price fixing, market allocation, tied financing, production cartels, and refusal to supply) do occur in Japan. That the executives believe the relative frequency of occurrence is greater than in the United States should be of no concern to the JFTC; if anticompetitive behavior occurs it warrants JFTC investigation regardless of the relative rate of activity in other countries. Likewise, that the responding executives sensed no negative impact on their business performance should be of no consequence to the JFTC. The AML is, first and foremost, intended to protect consumer interests. If proscribed behavior occurs, it may very well have a negative impact on consumer welfare regardless of the influence on competing businesses, and this alone justifies JFTC action.

As was discussed earlier, although businesses may be aware of anticompetitive behavior, and even possibly be harmed by it, they may still choose to remain silent due to legitimate concerns about potential retaliation or other adverse consequences to their existing business. This reticence need not be an insurmountable obstacle to the investigative duties of the JFTC. The foundation of antitrust legislation is its protection of consumers and businesses from unfair or anticompetitive practices exercised by those in positions of power relative to the victims. The apprehensions of those affected are justification for independent action by the JFTC, and their silence should not serve as a deterrent to corrective action.

Relative to its performance over the past 40 years, the JFTC has in the 1990s taken a more aggressive approach to enforcement of the AML. The Japanese government has acknowledged a need to enhance Japan's competitive environment and has pledged to support the JFTC's greater vigilance. This research verifies the legitimacy of the government's course.

QUALIFICATIONS AND LIMITATIONS

The survey sample included only large multinational U.S. companies that have the bulk of U.S. business experience operating in Japan and can speak most authoritatively about anticompetitive activities, but that also have the resources and power to most effectively deal with and minimize the impact of whatever anticompetitive behavior they may confront. These companies have established a critical presence in Japan and account for the bulk of U.S. goods exported and/or manufactured there. The survey did not include business firms that may have faced anticompetitive barriers so overwhelming that they either chose not to make an attempt or were compelled to abandon the effort. Such respondents may have expressed a very different opinion regarding the influence of anticompetitive behavior on their Japan operations.

Validation studies have found that executives' personal evaluations of performance are consistent with objective measures from internal or published information (Dess and Robinson 1984). However, there remains a possibility of overconfidence and overestimation in using self-assessments of business performance (Mahajan 1992). The measures of performance and competitive strength used in this study could be biased due to their reliance on executives' evaluations of their own company's accomplishments. In addition, executives may not be fully aware of the results achieved by their competitors, and therefore handicapped in estimating their own strengths and performance relative to their competitors. Unfortunately, performance figures specifically for the Japan operations (or any particular market) of the Fortune 500 companies surveyed are generally not public information. Only aggregated, worldwide sales and revenue statistics are published by these companies. To the extent that verifiable and objective measures of performance and competitive strength can be obtained, it could improve the quality of future research.

This research tested only the occurrence and impact of ten anticompetitive behaviors as defined by the JFTC. There are many other types of anticompetitive behavior, and other barriers to trade, that are alleged to exist and that deserve close empirical investigation. Likewise, this study addressed only manufactured goods. Complaints of anticompetitive behavior are common in some service sectors (e.g., construction and engineering, insurance, banking, and securities, legal services, transportation, shipping, banking, and securities) and in some markets for raw materials and commodities (e.g., soda ash and agricultural products). Further research is called for in these markets as well.

Appendix: Data Collection Questionnaire

PART 1: GENERAL GUIDELINES

This study investigates the interrelationships among market environment, strategies, and performance for U.S. companies marketing manufactured goods in Japan. Of course, these factors can vary across different business units of a company. Consequently, to help us gain a clear understanding of these relationships, please respond to the questions in this survey in reference to one particular business unit of your company. Please select a business unit which has considerable long-term significance to your company's objectives in Japan. If your company has more than one business unit, and you are willing to complete more than one questionnaire, your further cooperation will be much appreciated.

Accordingly, please indicate which particular business unit your response to the questions in this survey pertain to:

BUSINESS UNIT (Division): _____

Please respond to the following questions in reference to the above specified business unit's operations in Japan, unless otherwise stated. Please answer all questions to the best of your knowledge. If you wish to comment on any questions or qualify your answers, feel free to use the space in the margins or a separate sheet of paper.

All information that you provide will be kept strictly confidential and will be analyzed only at the aggregate level.

PART 2: MARKET ENVIRONMENT

The following questions (1–22) are concerned with recent characteristics of the market in which your business unit operates in Japan. On the following scale, please indicate the position that best describes your perception of these conditions.

	Very Low		Moderate		Very High
1. Market growth rate (1991–1993)	1	2	3	4	5
2. Intensity of price competition (1991–1993)	1	2	3	4	5
3. Average industry gross margins (1991–1993)	1	2	3	4	5
4. Average industry pretax profits (1991–1993)	1	2	3	3	5
5. Expected long-term (1991–2000) market growth rate	1	2	3	4	5
6. Outlook for future profits (1994–2000)	1	2	3	4	5
7. Market share concentration of the four largest companies in the market	1	2	3	4	5
8. Variety of substitute products	1	2	3	4	5
9. Number of component suppliers	1	2	3	4	5
10. Number of distributors	1	2	3	4	5

11. Number of competitors   1   2   3   4   5

12. Number of customers   1   2   3   4   5

	Very Low	Moderate	Very High

13. Capital investment required for your business unit to compete in Japan   1   2   3   4   5

14. One-time costs to a buyer due to switching from one supplier to another   1   2   3   4   5

15. Extent to which Japan's government limits or controls expansion in the market   1   2   3   4   5

	Much Lower	Same	Much Higher

16. Cost advantages of domestic (i.e., Japanese) competitors   1   2   3   4   5

17. Product differentiation offered by domestic (i.e., Japanese) competitors   1   2   3   4   5

18. In what stage of the product life cycle would you classify your business unit?

_____ Introduction   _____ Growth   _____ Early Maturity

_____ Late Maturity   _____ Decline

19. To what degree does local management control *product development* decisions for the Japan market (compared to the control exercised by your corporate headquarters)?

_____ Total Control   _____ Most Decisions _____ Equal Control

_____ Few Decisions   _____ No Control

20. To what degree does local management control *product pricing* decisions for the Japan market (compared to the control exercised by your corporate headquarters)?

_____ Total Control   _____ Most Decisions   _____ Equal Control

_____ Few Decisions   _____ No Control

21. To what degree does local management control *promotional* decisions for the Japan market (compared to the control exercised by your corporate headquarters)?

_____ Total Control   _____ Most Decisions   _____ Equal Control

_____ Few Decisions   _____ No Control

22. To what degree does local management control *investment* decisions for the Japan market (compared to the control exercised by your corporate headquarters)?

_____ Total Control   _____ Most Decisions   _____ Equal Control

_____ Few Decisions   _____ No Control

Questions 23–32 describe possible types of competitive behavior. For each case, please indicate your perception of the frequency of occurrence in Japan during the past *three years* (i.e., 1991–1993) *relative to* the frequency of occurrence in the United States. For example, if the behavior does not occur in either Japan or the United States, the relative frequency of occurrence, and the appropriate response, would be "Same." Please respond exclusively in reference only to the markets in which your business unit competes. Please note that you are not being asked to judge or comment upon the fairness or legality of these behaviors, only the frequency of occurrence relative to competitive behavior in your U.S. markets, and the degree of negative effect upon your business unit's performance in Japan.

23. A manufacturer informs independent distributors or end users that the manufacturer will not supply products if the distributors or end users purchase competing products.

	Much Less Often	Same	Much More Often
Occurrence in Japan relative to the U.S.	1 2	3	4 5

	Strongly Disagree				Strongly Agree

The occurrence of this behavior in Japan has had a negative effect on the performance of our business unit.

1 2 3 4 5

24. Manufacturers or distributors inform independent suppliers that they will discontinue purchases if the suppliers sell materials to competing businesses.

	Much Less Often		Same		Much More Often

Occurrence in Japan relative to the U.S.

1 2 3 4 5

	Strongly Disagree				Strongly Agree

The occurrence of this behavior in Japan has had a negative effect on the performance of our business unit.

1 2 3 4 5

25. A group of manufacturers or distributors mutually arranges not to deal with each other's customers.

	Much Less Often		Same		Much More Often

Occurrence in Japan relative to the U.S.

1 2 3 4 5

	Strongly Disagree				Strongly Agree

The occurrence of this behavior in Japan has had a negative effect on the performance of our business unit.

1 2 3 4 5

26. A financial firm provides financing for a distributor or end user on the condition that the recipient deals exclusively with a manufacturer who has a relationship with the financial firm.

	Much Less Often	Same	Much More Often

Occurrence in Japan relative
to the U.S.   1   2   3   4   5

	Strongly Disagree		Strongly Agree

The occurrence of this behavior
in Japan has had a negative effect
on the performance of
our business unit.   1   2   3   4   5

27. A manufacturer causes an independent distributor to restrict
     promotion of a new product until the manufacturer develops
     a competitive product.

	Much Less Often	Same	Much More Often

Occurrence in Japan relative
to the U.S.   1   2   3   4   5

	Strongly Disagree		Strongly Agree

The occurrence of this behavior
in Japan has had a negative effect
on the performance of
our business unit.   1   2   3   4   5

28. A manufacturer agrees to repurchase from a retailer unsold
     inventory at the price paid by the retailer on condition that
     the retailer maintains the manufacturer's suggested retail
     price.

	Much Less Often	Same	Much More Often

Occurrence in Japan relative
to the U.S.   1   2   3   4   5

	Strongly Disagree			Strongly Agree

The occurrence of this behavior
in Japan has had a negative effect
on the performance of
our business unit.

| 1 | 2 | 3 | 4 | 5 |

29. A manufacturer threatens to withdraw its advertisements unless advertisements for a competing product are rejected.

	Much Less Often		Same	Much More Often

Occurrence in Japan relative
to the U.S.

| 1 | 2 | 3 | 4 | 5 |

	Strongly Disagree			Strongly Agree

The occurrence of this behavior
in Japan has had a negative effect
on the performance of
our business unit.

| 1 | 2 | 3 | 4 | 5 |

30. A group of manufacturers mutually agree to fix the price of a product.

	Much Less Often		Same	Much More Often

Occurrence in Japan relative
to the U.S.

| 1 | 2 | 3 | 4 | 5 |

	Strongly Disagree			Strongly Agree

The occurrence of this behavior
in Japan has had a negative effect
on the performance of
our business unit.

| 1 | 2 | 3 | 4 | 5 |

31. A group of manufacturers mutually agree to restrict production and supply of a product.

	Much Less Often	Same	Much More Often	
Occurrence in Japan relative to the U.S.	1	2	3	4	5

	Strongly Disagree		Strongly Agree	
The occurrence of this behavior in Japan has had a negative effect on the performance of our business unit.	1	2	3	4	5

32. Companies bidding for a specific project hold mutual consult-ations prior to the bidding to determine which company will win the contract.

	Much Less Often	Same	Much More Often	
Occurrence in Japan relative to the U.S.	1	2	3	4	5

	Strongly Disagree		Strongly Agree	
The occurrence of this behavior in Japan has had a negative effect on the performance of our business unit	1	2	3	4	5

PART 3: RELATIVE COMPETITIVE STRENGTH

The following questions are concerned with the competitive strength of your business unit. Please indicate the position that best describes your perception of your business unit's competitive strength in Japan *relative to* your competitors (domestic and foreign).

1. Please rate your business unit on the following dimensions, *relative to* your major competitors in Japan:

	Much Lower		Same		Much Better
Product differentiation	1	2	3	4	5
Initiating product improvements	1	2	3	4	5
Breadth of product line	1	2	3	4	5
Competitive pricing	1	2	3	4	5
Technological innovation	1	2	3	4	5
Quality of service	1	2	3	4	5
Service improvements	1	2	3	4	5
Salesforce effectiveness	1	2	3	4	5
Company image	1	2	3	4	5
Bargaining position with customers	1	2	3	4	5
Economies of scale	1	2	3	4	5
Market share	1	2	3	4	5
Ability to gain market share	1	2	3	4	5
Pretax profitability	1	2	3	4	5
Promotional practices	1	2	3	4	5

PART 4: STRATEGIC MARKETING OBJECTIVES

The following questions are concerned with the strategic objectives and actions of your business unit in Japan *during the past three years* (i.e., 1991–1993). Please indicate the position that best describes the strategic marketing objectives and actions of your business unit in Japan.

	Strongly Disagree				Strongly Agree
1. It has been our objective to increase our market share in Japan.	1	2	3	4	5

2. We increased our investment
   in resources dedicated to
   serving our customers in Japan. 1   2   3   4   5

3. We set aggressive sales goals
   for our operations in Japan.   1   2   3   4   5

4. We heavily promoted
   our products in Japan.   1   2   3   4   5

5. We initiated product changes
   to better adapt our products
   to the needs and demands of
   our Japanese customers.   1   2   3   4   5

6. Our business motivation to operate in
   Japan during the past three years
   (i.e., 1991–1993) has been:

to compete against our Japanese
competitors in their own market   1   2   3   4   5

to improve our product quality   1   2   3   4   5

to establish a strategic outpost
for future growth   1   2   3   4   5

to develop a global sourcing site   1   2   3   4   5

to increase our worldwide sales
revenues   1   2   3   4   5

to increase our global market
share   1   2   3   4   5

to improve our profitability   1   2   3   4   5

to improve our worldwide
competitive strength   1   2   3   4   5

to improve our technology   1   2   3   4   5

to achieve greater economies
of scale   1   2   3   4   5

PART 5: BUSINESS PERFORMANCE

The following questions are concerned with your business unit's performance and future outlook. Please indicate the position that best describes the performance of your business unit *relative to your three largest competitors in Japan*

1. Over the past three years, and relative to our three largest competitors, our business unit's performance in Japan on the following dimensions has been:

	Much Lower		Same		Much Higher
Market share	1	2	3	4	5
Sales growth rate	1	2	3	4	5
Pretax profits	1	2	3	4	5
Return on investment	1	2	3	4	5
Product quality	1	2	3	4	5
Service quality	1	2	3	4	5
Customer satisfaction	1	2	3	4	5

2. Relative to our three largest competitors, our business unit's likelihood of improvement during the next three years on each of the following dimensions is:

	Much Lower		Same		Much Higher
Market share	1	2	3	4	5
Sales growth rate	1	2	3	4	5
Pretax profits	1	2	3	4	5
Return on investment	1	2	3	4	5
Product quality	1	2	3	4	5
Service quality	1	2	3	4	5
Customer satisfaction	1	2	3	4	5

PART 6: BUSINESS UNIT'S CHARACTERISTICS

The following questions are concerned with general information about your business unit's history in Japan, general characteristics of your company, and yourself.

1. Number of years your business unit has operated in Japan.

— 0–5 yrs   — 6–10 yrs   — 11–15 yrs   — 16–20 yrs   — More than 20

2. Approximate dollar value of your unit's sales in Japan as a percentage of your unit's (i.e., worldwide) sales in FY1993.

— 0–5%   — 6–10%   — 11–15%   — 16–20%   — More than 20%

3. Your company's total (i.e., worldwide) sales in FY1993, in billions of U.S. dollars.

$____

4. Which of the following best describes the products of your business unit?

_____ Consumer goods   _____ Industrial goods

5. The industry in which your business unit operates is best described as:

— Aerospace	— Forest Products	— Publishing, Printing
— Apparel	— Furniture	— Rubber & Plastic Product
— Beverages	— Industrial & Farm Eqp	— Scientific & Photo Eqp
— Building Materials	— Metal & Metal Prod	— Soaps, Cosmetics
— Chemicals	— Mining, Crud Oil Prod	— Textiles
— Computers/Office	— Motor Vehicles & Parts	— Tobacco
— Electronics	— Petroleum Refining	— Toys, Sporting Goods
— Food	— Pharmaceutical	— Transportation Eqp
— Other		

6. How many years have you personally been involved with business in Japan?

___ 0–5 yrs   ___ 6–10 yrs   ___ 16–20 yrs   ___ 11–15 yrs   ___ More than 20

7. How many years have you worked for this company?

___ 0–5 yrs   ___ 6–10 yrs   ___ 11–15 yrs   ___ 16–20 yrs   ___ More than 20

8. What is your nationality?

___ American   ___ Japanese   ___ Other

Thank you very much for your time and cooperation!

Would you like a summary copy of the results of this survey?

_____ Yes _____ No

Name & Address: _____

_____

_____

_____

Bibliography

Aaby, Nils-Erik, and Stanley F. Slater (1989), "Management Influences on Export Performance: A Review of the Empirical Literature 1978–88," *International Marketing Review*, 6, no. 4, pp. 7–26.

Abegglen, James, and George Stalk, Jr. (1985), *Kaisha: The Japanese Corporation*, New York: Basic Books.

Alden, Vernon R. (1985), "Who Says You Can't Crack Japanese Markets," *Harvard Business Review*, 65 (January-February), pp. 52–56.

Allen, M. George (1994), "Succeeding in Japan: One Company's Perspective," *Vital Speeches of the Day* 60, no. 14 (May 1), pp. 429–432.

American Chamber of Commerce in Japan (1991), *Trade and Investment in Japan: The Current Environment*, prepared by A. T. Kearney, Tokyo: ACCJ.

American Chamber of Commerce in Japan (1993), *1993 Trade White Paper*, Tokyo: ACCJ.

Anchordoguy, Marie (1989), *Computers, Inc.: Japan's Challenge to IBM*, Cambridge, Mass.: Harvard University Press.

Anchordoguy, Marie (1990), "A Challenge to Free Trade? Japanese Industrial Targeting in the Computer and Semiconductor Industries," in *Japan's Economic Structure: Should It Change?* edited by Kozo Yamamura, Seattle: Society for Japanese Studies, University of Washington, pp. 301–332.

Atwood, James R. (1984), "Extraterritorial Discovery: The Special Case of Antitrust," in *Extraterritorial Discovery in International Litigation,* edited by Selvyn Seidel, New York: Practicing Law Institute, pp. 319–360.

Bain, Joe S. (1959), *Industrial Organization,* New York: John Wiley and Sons Inc.

Bain, Joe S., and P. David Qualls (1987), *Industrial Organization: A Treatise,* Greenwich, Conn.: JAI Press.

Balassa, Bela (1986), "Japan's Trade Policies," *Weltwirtschaftliches Archiv,* 122, no. 4, pp. 745–790.

Balassa, Bela, and Marcus Noland (1988), *Japan in the World Economy,* Washington, D. C.: Institute for International Economics.

Bauerschmidt, Alan, Daniel Sullivan, and Kate Gillespie (1985), "Common Factors Underlying Barriers to Export: Studies in the U.S. Paper Industry," *Journal of International Business Studies,* 16 (Fall), pp. 111–123.

Baumol, William J., and Janusz A. Ordover (1985), "Use of Antitrust to Subvert Competition," *Journal of Law and Economics,* 28 (May), pp. 247–265.

Bergsten, C. Fred, and William R. Cline (1985), *The United States-Japan Economic Problem*: *Policy Analyses in International Economics,* 13 (October), Washington, D.C.: Institute for International Economics.

Bergsten, C. Fred, and Marcus Noland (1993), *Irreconcilable Differences?* Washington, D.C.: Institute for International Economics.

Bhagwati, Jagdish (1994), "Samurais No More," *Foreign Affairs,* 73, no. 3 (May/June), pp. 7–12.

Bilkey, Warren J. (1982), "Variables Associated with Export Profitability," *Journal of International Business Studies,* 13 (Fall), pp. 39–55.

Bilkey, Warren J. (1985), "Development of Export Marketing Guidelines," *International Marketing Review,* 2, no. 1 (Spring), pp. 31–40.

Bock, Betty (1981), "Overview," in *Antitrust in the Competitive World of the 1980's: Exploring Options,* edited by Betty Bock et al., The Conference Board, Antitrust Forum 1981, Research Bulletin, no. 112, pp. 3–10.

Bork, Robert H. (1978), *The Antitrust Paradox,* New York: Basic Books.

Boudin, Michael (1990), "American Antitrust Abroad: The Problem of Foreign Private Restraints on U.S. Exports," in *Federal Antitrust Enforcement in the 90s,* edited by Judy Whalley and Christian White, vol. 2, New York: Practicing Law Institute, pp. 17–31.

Brouthers, Lance Eliot, and Steve Werner (1990), "Are the Japanese Good Global Competitors?" *Columbia Journal of World Business*, 25 (Fall), pp. 5–11.

Buckley, Peter J., and Mark Casson (1976), *The Future of the Multinational Enterprise*, London: MacMillan.

Burke, Marian C. (1984), "Strategic Choice and Marketing Managers: An Examination of Business-Level Marketing Objectives," *Journal of Marketing Research*, 21 (November), pp. 345–359.

Buzzell, Robert (1968), "Can You Standardize Multinational Marketing?" *Harvard Business Review*, 46 (November/December), pp. 102–113.

Buzzell, Robert D., and Bradley T. Gale (1987), *The PIMS Principles*, New York: Free Press.

Casson, Mark (1979), *Alternatives to Multinational Enterprise*, New York: Holmes and Meier.

Caves, R. E., and M. E. Porter (1977), "From Entry Barriers to Mobility Barriers: Conjectural Decisions and Contrived Deterrence to New Competition," *Quarterly Journal of Economics*, 91 (May), pp. 241–261.

Cavusgil, S. Tamer, and V. H. Kirpalani (1993), "Introducing Products into Export Markets: Success Factors," *Journal of Business Research*, 27, pp. 1–15.

Cavusgil, S. Tamer, and John R. Nevin (1981), "Internal Determinants of Export Marketing Behavior: An Empirical Investigation," *Journal of Marketing Research*, 18, pp. 114–119.

Cavusgil, S. Tamer, and Shaoming Zou (1994), "Marketing Strategy-Performance Relationship: An Investigation of the Empirical Link in Export Market Ventures," *Journal of Marketing*, 58 (January), pp. 1–21.

Choate, Pat (1990), *Agents of Influence*, New York: Alfred A. Knopf.

Christensen, C. H., A. da Rocha, and R. K. Gertner (1987), "An Empirical Investigation of the Factors Influencing Exporting Success of Brazilian Firms," *Journal of International Business Studies*, 18 (Fall), pp. 61–77.

Christopher, Robert C. (1983), *The Japanese Mind*, New York: Linden Press.

Christopher, Warren (1994), "The Responsibility to Change: United States-Japan Relations," *Vital Speeches of the Day*, 60, no. 12 (April 1), pp. 360–363.

Clark, Rodney (1979), *The Japanese Company*, New Haven, Conn.: Yale University Press.

Cline, William R. (1983), "Reciprocity: A New Approach to World Trade Policy?" in *Trade Policy in the 1980s*, edited by William R. Cline, Washington, D.C.: Institute for International Economics.

Cline, William R. (1990), "Japan's Trade Policies," a paper delivered to the MITI Research Institute, Tokyo (May).

Cook, Victor J. Jr. (1983), "Marketing Strategy and Differential Advantage," *Journal of Marketing*, 47 (Spring), pp. 68–75.

Cooper, R. G., and E. J. Kleinschmidt (1985), "The Impact of Export Strategy on Export Sales Performance," *Journal of International Business Studies*, 16 (Spring), pp. 37–55.

Coughlan, Anne T., and Lisa K. Scheer (1987), "Keiretsu Strength in Japanese Industrial Organization: Empirical Evidence on the Decision Participation Framework," Working Paper, Northwestern University.

Craig, C. Samuel, Susan P. Douglas, and Srinivas K. Reddy (1987), "Market Structure, Performance and Strategy: A Comparison of U.S. and European Markets," *Advances in International Marketing*, 2, pp. 1–21.

Cutts, Robert L. (1992), "Capitalism in Japan: Cartels and Keiretsu," *Harvard Business Review*, 70 (July-August), pp. 48–55.

Czinkota, Michael R., and Masaaki Kotabe (1993), "Distribution and Trade Relations Between the United States and Japan: An Overview and Assessment," in *The Japanese Distribution System*, edited by Michael R. Czinkota and Masaaki Kotabe, Chicago: Probus, pp. 5–19.

Daily Yomiuri (1991), "Glass, Paper New Sources of Friction," December 17.

Daily Yomiuri (1992a), "EC Accuses Japanese of Abusing GATT Rules," July 14.

Daily Yomiuri (1992b), "Plastic Wrap Companies Call Indictment Unjust," May 15.

Daily Yomiuri (1993), "Ministry Set to Publish Importers' Cost Prices," September 10.

Daily Yomiuri (1994a), "Clinton Slams Japan Markets," March 10.

Daily Yomiuri (1994b), "Construction Giants Define Dango as 'Beneficial'," March 15.

Datta, Deepak K., and John H. Grant (1990), "Relationships Between Type of Acquisition, the Autonomy Given to the Acquired Firm, and Acquisition Success: An Empirical Analysis," *Journal of Management*, 16, no. 1, pp. 29–44.

Davidson, William H. (1980), *Experience Effects in International Investment and Technology Transfer*, Ann Arbor, Mich.: UMI Research Press.

Davidson, William H. (1983), *The Amazing Race: Winning the Technorivalry with Japan*, New York: John Wiley and Son.

Day, George S., and Robin Wensley (1988), "Assessing Advantage: A Framework for Diagnosing Competitive Superiority," *Journal of Marketing*, 52 (April), pp. 1–20.

Debow, Michael E. (1990), "Do Not Use U.S. Antitrust Enforcement to Promote U.S. Exports," *Regulation*, 13, no. 3 (Fall), pp. 16–18.

DeMente, Boye (1981), *The Japanese Way of Doing Business*, Englewood Cliffs, NJ: Prentice-Hall.

Dess, G. G., and Richard B. Robinson (1984), "Measuring Organizational Performance in the Absence of Objective Measures: The Case of the Privately Held Firm and Conglomerate Business Unit," *Strategic Management Journal*, 5, pp. 265–273.

DiLorenzo, Thomas J. (1990), "The Origins of Antitrust: Rhetoric vs. Reality," *Regulation*, Fall, pp. 26–34.

Dosi, Giovanni, Laura D'Andrea Tyson, and John Zysman (1989), "Trade Technologies and Development: A Framework for Discussing Japan," in *Politics and Productivity: The Real Story of Why Japan Works*, edited by Chalmers Johnson, Laura D'Andrea Tyson, and John Zysman, Cambridge, Mass.: Ballinger.

Douglas, Susan P., and C. Samuel Craig (1989), "Evolution of Global Marketing Strategy: Scale, Scope and Synergy," *Columbia Journal of World Business* (Fall), pp. 47–58.

Doyle, Peter, John Saunders, and Veronica Wong (1992), "Competition in Global Markets: A Case Study of American and Japanese Competition in the British Market," *Journal of International Business Studies*, 23 (Third Quarter), pp. 419–442.

Drucker, Peter F. (1994), "Trade Lessons from the World Economy," *Foreign Affairs*, 73, no. 1 (January/February), pp. 99–108.

Dunning, John H. (1977), "Trade, Location of Economic Activity and the MNE: A Search for an Eclectic Approach," in *The International Allocation of Economic Activity*, edited by Bertil Ohlin, Per-Ove Hesselborn, and Per Magnus Wijkman, New York: Holms and Meier, pp. 395–418.

Eads, George C., and Kozo Yamamura (1987), "The Future of Industrial Policy," in *The Political Economy of Japan: The Domestic Transformation*, edited by Kozo Yamamura and Yasukichi Yasuba, Stanford, Calif.: Stanford University Press.

Economist (1989), "Japanese Distribution: Too Many Shopkeepers," January 28, pp. 70–71.

Economist (1991a), "Communities of Interest," April 27, pp. 36–37.

Economist (1991b), "Japan's Next Retail Revolution," December 21, pp. 81–82.

Einhorn, Hillel J., and Robin M. Hogarth (1981), "Behavioral Decision Theory: Processes of Judgment and Choice," *Annual Review of Psychology*, 32, pp. 53–88.

Encarnation, Dennis J. (1992), *Rivals Beyond Trade: America versus Japan in Global Competition*, Ithaca, N.Y.: Cornell University Press.

Fair Trade Commission (1991), *The Antimonopoly Act Guidelines Concerning Distribution Systems and Business Practices*, Tokyo: Executive Office of the Fair Trade Commission of Japan.

Fair Trade Commission (1992), *The Outline of the Report on the Actual Conditions of the Six Major Corporate Groups*, Tokyo: Executive Office of the Fair Trade Commission of Japan, February.

Fallows, James (1989), "Containing Japan," *Atlantic Monthly*, May, pp. 40–54.

Fallows, James (1993), "Looking at the Sun," *Atlantic Monthly*, November, pp. 69–100.

Far Eastern Economic Review (1989), "Japan's Price Fixers," June 8, p. 101.

Far Eastern Economic Review (1992), "Stones Through Glass," June 18, pp. 80–81.

Fenwick, Ian, and Lyn Amine (1979), "Export Performance and Export Policy: Evidence from the U.K. Clothing Industry," *Journal of the Operational Research Society*, 30, no. 8, pp. 747–754.

Final Report on the SII Talks (1990), jointly published by the governments of Japan and the United States, June 28.

First Annual Report of SII Follow-Up (1991), jointly published by the governments of Japan and the United States, May 22.

First, Harry (1986), "Japan's Antitrust Policy: Impact on Import Competition," in *Fragile Interdependence: Economic Issues in U.S.-Japan Trade and Investment*, edited by Thomas A. Pugel and Robert G. Hawkins, New York: Center for Japan-U.S. Business and Economics, New York University, pp. 63–76.

First, Harry (1993), "Selling Antitrust in Japan," *Antitrust*, Spring, pp. 34–37.

Flath, David (1993), "Shareholding in the Keiretsu, Japan's Financial Groups," *Review of Economics and Statistics*, 75, no. 2 (May), pp. 249–257.

Fortune (1986), "Are Japanese Managers Biased Against Americans?" September 1, pp. 72–75.

Frost, Ellen L. (1987), *For Richer, For Poorer*, Washington, D.C.: Council on Foreign Relations.

Fugate, Wilbur L. (1983), "Antitrust Aspects of U.S.-Japanese Trade," *Case Western Reserve Journal of International Law*, 15, pp. 505–525.

Fugate, Wilbur L. (1991), *Foreign Commerce and the Antitrust Laws*, 4th ed., Boston: Little, Brown.

Fujigane, Yasuo, and Peter Ennis (1990), *"Keiretsu*: What They Are Doing; Where They Are Heading," *Tokyo Business Today*, September, pp. 26–30.

Fung, K. C. (1991), "Characteristics of Japanese Industrial Groups and Their Potential Impact on U.S.-Japan Trade," in *Empirical Studies of Commercial Policy*, edited by Robert Baldwin, Chicago: University of Chicago Press.

Gellhorn, Ernest, Charles A. James, Richard Pogue, and Joe Sims (1990), "Has Antitrust Outgrown Dual Enforcement? A Proposal for Rationalization," *Antitrust Bulletin*, 35, no. 3 (Fall), pp. 695–743.

Gerlach, Michael L. (1989), *"Keiretsu* Organization in the Japanese Economy," in *Politics and Productivity: The Real Story of Why Japan Works*, edited by Chalmers Johnson, Laura D'Andrea Tyson, and John Zysman, Cambridge, Mass.: Ballinger.

Gerlach, Michael L. (1992), "Twilight of the *Keiretsu*? A Critical Assessment," *Journal of Japanese Studies*, 18, no.1, pp. 79–118.

Gibney, Frank (1975), *Japan: The Fragile Superpower*, Rutland, Vt.: Charles E. Tuttle.

Ginsburg, Douglas H. (1991), "Antitrust as Antimonopoly," *Regulation*, Summer, pp. 91–100.

Glazer, Rashi, and Allen M. Weiss (1993), "Marketing in Turbulent Environments: Decision Processes and the Time-Sensitivity of Information," *Journal of Marketing Research*, 30 (November), pp. 509–521.

Glejser, Herbert, Alexis Jacquemin, and Jean Petit (1980), "Exports in Imperfect Competition Framework: An Analysis of 1,446 Exporters," *Quarterly Journal of Economics*, 94 (May), pp. 507–524.

Graglia, Lino A. (1991), "One Hundred Years of Antitrust," *Public Interest*, 104 (Summer), pp. 50–66.

Graham, Edward M, and Paul R. Krugman (1989), *Foreign Direct Investment in the United States*, Washington, D.C.: Institute for International Economics.

Green, Robert T., and Trina L. Larsen (1987), "Only Retaliation Will Open up Japan," *Harvard Business Review*, 65 (November-December), pp. 22–28.

Hadley, Eleanor M. (1970), *Antitrust in Japan*, Princeton, N.J.: Princeton University Press.

Haitani, Kanji (1976), *The Japanese Economic System*, Lexington, Mass.: Lexington Books.

Haley, John O. (1978), "The Myth of the Reluctant Litigant," *Journal of Japanese Studies*, 4, p. 359–390.

Haley, John O. (1982), "Sheathing the Sword of Justice in Japan: An Essay on Law Without Sanctions," *Journal of Japanese Studies*, 8, no. 2, pp. 267–281.

Haley, John O. (1984), "Antitrust Sanctions and Remedies: A Comparative Study of German and Japanese Law," *Washington Law Review*, vol. 59, pp. 471–508.

Haley, John O. (1990), "Weak Law, Strong Competition, and Trade Barriers: Competitiveness as a Disincentive to Foreign Entry into Japanese Markets," in *Japan's Economic Structure: Should It Change?* edited by Kozo Yamamura, Seattle: Society for Japanese Studies, University of Washington, pp. 203–235.

Haley, John O. (1991), "Japanese Antitrust Enforcement: Implications for United States Trade," *Northern Kentucky Law Review*, 18, no. 3, pp. 335–366.

Harrigan, James (1993), "OECD Imports and Trade Barriers in 1983," *Journal of International Economics*, 35, no. 1/2 (August), pp. 91–111.

Heckscher, Eli F, and Bertil Ohlin (1991), *Heckscher-Ohlin Trade Theory*, translated, edited, and introduced by Harry Flam and M. June Flanders, Cambridge, Mass.: MIT Press.

Heflebower, R. B. (1960), "Observations of Decentralization in Large Enterprises," *Journal of Industrial Economics*, 9, no. 2, pp. 7–22.

Helms, Leslie (1991), "Japan Lashes Out," *Daily Yomiuri*, October 29 (originally appearing in the *Los Angeles Times*).

Helpman, Elhanan, and Paul R. Krugman (1985), *Market Structure and Foreign Trade*, Cambridge, Mass.: MIT Press.

Henderson, Dan F. (1986), "Access to the Japanese Market: Some Aspects of Foreign Exchange Controls and Banking Law," in *Law and Trade Issues of the Japanese Economy: American and Japanese Perspectives*, edited by Gary R. Saxonhouse and Kozo Yamamura, Seattle: University of Washington Press, pp. 131–156.

Hills, Carla A. (1981), "Private Enforcement and Public Policy," in *Antitrust in the Competitive World of the 1980's: Exploring Options*, edited by Betty Bock et al., The Conference Board, Antitrust Forum 1981, Research Bulletin no. 112, pp. 18–20.

Holstein, William J. (1990), *The Japanese Power Game: What It Means for America*, New York: Charles Scribner's Sons.

Iacocca, Lee (1992), "Taking Care of Business: The Japanese Must Open Their Markets," *Vital Speeches of the Day*, 58, no. 10, pp. 295–299.

Imai, Ken-Ichi (1990), "Japanese Business Groups and the Structural Impediments Initiative," in *Japan's Economic Structure: Should It*

Change? edited by Kozo Yamamura, Seattle: Society for Japanese Studies, University of Washington, pp. 167–202.

International Herald Tribune (1993), "8 Firms Are Fined in Tokyo for Cartel," May 22.

Irwin, Douglas (1994), *Mismanaged Trade: The Case Against Import Targets*, Washington, D.C.: American Enterprise Institute, June.

Ishihara, Shintaro (1989), *The Japan That Can Say No*, New York: Simon and Schuster.

Ishikawa, Tadashi (1989), "Antitrust Enforcement by the Japan Fair Trade Commission," *Antitrust*, Summer, pp. 11–15.

Itoh, Motoshige, Kazuharu Kiyono, Masahiro Okuno-Fujiwara, and Kotaro Suzumura (1991), *Economic Analysis of Industrial Policy*, translated by Anil Khosla, New York: Academic Press.

Jacobson, Robert, and David A. Aaker (1987), "The Strategic Role of Product Quality," *Journal of Marketing*, 51 (Fall), pp. 31–44.

Jain, Subhash C. (1989), "Standardization of International Marketing Strategy: Some Research Hypotheses," *Journal of Marketing*, 53 (January), pp. 70–79.

Japan Economic Institute (1990), "Japan's Price Structure," *JEI Report*, 4A, January 26.

Japan Times (1990), "Inept Reaction to Revisionists," January 13.

Japan Times (1992), "Firms Told to Ease Trade Tensions by Cooperating with Foreign Rivals," May 28.

Jatusripitak, Somkid, Liam Fahey, and Philip Kotler (1985), "Strategic Global Marketing: Lessons from the Japanese," *Columbia Journal of World Business*, 20 (Spring), pp. 47–53.

Johns, B. L. (1962), "Barriers to Entry in a Dynamic Setting," *Journal of Industrial Economics*, 11 (November), pp. 48–61.

Johnson, Chalmers (1982), *MITI and the Japanese Economic Miracle*, Stanford, Calif.: Stanford University Press.

Johnson, Chalmers (1990a), "*Keiretsu*: An Outsider's View," *Economic Insight*, 1, no. 2 (September/October), pp. 15–17.

Johnson, Chalmers (1990b), "Trade, Revisionism, and the Future of Japanese-American Relations," in *Japan's Economic Structure: Should It Change?* edited by Kozo Yamamura, Seattle: Society for Japanese Studies, University of Washington, pp. 105–136.

Johnson, Chalmers, Laura D'Andrea Tyson, and John Zysman, eds. (1989), *Politics and Productivity: The Real Story of Why Japan Works*, Cambridge, Mass.: Ballinger.

Kahn, Herman, and Thomas Pepper (1980), *The Japanese Challenge: The Success and Failure of Economic Success*, New York: William Morrow.

Karakaya, Fahri, and Michael J. Stahl (1989), "Barriers to Entry and Market Entry Decisions in Consumer and Industrial Goods Markets," *Journal of Marketing*, 53 (April), pp. 80–91.

Kedia, B. L. and J. Chokar (1986), "Factors Inhibiting Export Performance of Firms: An Empirical Investigation," *Management International Review*, 26, no. 4, pp. 33–43.

Keidanren (1990a), *Keidanren Position Paper on the Structural Impediments Initiative (SII) Talks*, Takyo: Keidanren, March 13.

Keidanren (1990b), "Views on Japan's Distribution System: Keidanren Suggestions in the Context of the SII Talks," *KKC Brief*, no. 58 (July), Keizai Koho Center.

Keidanren (1991), "Following Through on the Structural Impediments Initiative," *Economic Eye*, 12, no. 3 (Autumn), pp. 23–27.

Kogut, Bruce (1985), "Designing Global Strategies: Comparative and Competitive Value-Added Chains," *Sloan Management Review*, 26 (Summer), pp. 15–28.

Kojima, Kiyoshi, and Terutomo Ozawa (1984), *Japan's General Trading Companies: Merchants of Economic Development*, Paris: OECD.

Komiya, Ryutaro, Masahiro Okuno, and Kotaro Suzumura, eds., (1988), *Industrial Policy in Japan*, translated under the supervision of Kazuo Sato, New York: Academic Press.

Kotabe, Masaaki (1984), "Changing Roles of the Sogo Shoshas, the Manufacturing Firms, and the MITI in the Context of the Japanese 'Trade or Die' Mentality," *Columbia Journal of World Business*, 19 (Fall), pp. 33–42.

Kotabe, Masaaki (1989), "How Cooperative Are Member Companies in a Japanese Industrial Group? A Sourcing Transaction Perspective," paper presented at the Second Annual Conference of the Association of Japanese Business Studies, January.

Kotabe, Masaaki (1990), "Corporate Product Policy and Innovative Behavior of European and Japanese Multinationals: An Empirical Investigation," *Journal of Marketing*, 54 (April), pp. 19–33.

Kotabe, Masaaki (1992), *Global Sourcing Strategy: R&D, Manufacturing, and Marketing Interfaces*, New York: Quorum.

Kotabe, Masaaki, and Dale F. Duhan (1991), "The Perceived Veracity of PIMS Strategy Principles in Japan: An Empirical Inquiry," *Journal of Marketing*, 55 (January), pp. 26–41.

Kotler, Philip, Liam Fahey, and Somkid Jatusripitak (1985), *The New Competition*, Englewood Cliffs, N.J.: Prentice-Hall.

Krattenmaker, Thomas G., and Steven C. Salop (1987), "Exclusion and Antitrust," *Regulation*, 10, no.3/4, pp. 29–33, 40.

Kreinin, Mordechai E. (1988), "How Closed Is Japan's Market? Additional Evidence," *World Economy*, 11 (December), pp. 529–542.

Krugman, Paul R. (1987a), "Is the Japan Problem Over?" in *Trade Friction and Economic Policy: Problems and Prospects for Japan and the United States*, edited by Ryuzo Sato and Paul Wachtel, Cambridge: Cambridge University Press, pp. 16–44.

Krugman, Paul R. (1987b), "Targeted Industrial Policies: Theory and Evidence," in *The New Protectionist Threat to World Welfare*, edited by Dominick Salvatore, New York: Elsevier Science Publishing, pp. 266–296.

Krugman, Paul R. (1994), "Competitiveness: A Dangerous Obsession," *Foreign Affairs*, 73, no. 2 (March/April), pp. 28–44.

Krugman, Paul R., ed., (1991), *Trade with Japan: Has the Door Opened Wider?* Chicago: National Bureau of Economic Research, University of Chicago Press.

Kuriyama, Takakazu (1994), "U.S. and Japan Trade Relations: Japan Has Barriers as Does the U.S.," *Vital Speeches of the Day*, 60, no. 14 (May 1), pp. 421–424.

Lawrence, Paul R., and Jay W. Lorsch (1967), *Organization and Environment*, Homewood, Ill.: Irwin.

Lawrence, Robert Z. (1987), "Imports in Japan: Closed Markets or Minds?" *Brookings Papers on Economic Activity*, 2, pp. 517–548.

Lawrence, Robert Z. (1991a), "Efficient or Exclusionist? The Import Behavior of Japanese Corporate Groups," *Brookings Papers on Economic Activity*, 1, pp. 311–341.

Lawrence, Robert Z. (1991b), "How Open Is Japan?" in *Trade with Japan: Has the Door Opened Wider?* edited by Paul Krugman, Chicago: National Bureau of Economic Research, University of Chicago Press, pp. 9–37.

Lawrence, Robert Z., and Charles L. Schultze (1990), *An American Trade Strategy: Options for the 1990s*, Washington, D.C.: Brookings Institution.

Lazer, William, Shoji Murata, and Hiroshi Kosaka (1985), "Japanese Marketing: Towards a Better Understanding," *Journal of Marketing*, 49 (Spring), pp. 69–81.

Leamer, Edward E. (1988), "Measures of Openness," in *Trade Policy Issues and Empirical Analysis*, edited by R. E. Baldwin, Chicago: University of Chicago Press, pp. 147–204.

Leamer, Edward E. (1991), "Empirical Studies of Trade Issues: The Structure and Effects of Tariff and Non-Tariff Barriers in 1983," in *Political Economy of International Trade: Essays in Honor of Robert E. Baldwin*, edited by Ronald Jones and Anne Krueger, Cambridge, Mass.: Basil Blackwell.

Levitt, Theodore (1983), "The Globalization of Markets," *Harvard Business Review*, 61 (May-June), pp. 92–102.

Liebeler, Wesley J. (1987), "Exclusion or Efficiency," *Regulation*, 10, no. 3/4, pp. 34–40.

Lincoln, Edward J. (1984), *Japan's Industrial Policies*, Washington, D.C.: Japan Economic Institute (April).

Lincoln, Edward J. (1990), *Japan's Unequal Trade*, Washington, D.C.: Brookings Institution.

Lipsky, Abbott B. Jr. (1991), "Current Developments in Japanese Competition Law: Antimonopoly Act Enforcement Guidelines Resulting from the Structural Impediments Initiative," *Antitrust Law Journal*, 60, pp. 279–289.

Loertscher, Rudolf, and Frank Wolter (1980), "Determinants of Intra-Industry Trade: Among Countries and Across Industries," *Weltwirtschaftliches Archiv*, 116, no. 2, pp. 280–293.

Madsen, Tage K. (1987), "Empirical Export Performance Studies: A Review of Conceptualizations and Findings," in *Advances in International Marketing*, vol. 2, edited by S. Tamer Cavusgil, Greenwich, Conn.: JAI Press, pp. 177–198.

Magney, John S. (1992), "U.S. Extends Reach of Antitrust Enforcement," *International Financial Law Review*, 11, no. 6 (June), pp. 18–21.

Mahajan, Jayashree (1992), "The Overconfidence Effect in Marketing Management Predictions," *Journal of Marketing Research*, 29 (August), pp. 329–342.

Mainichi Daily News (1993a), "Four Printing Companies Found Guilty in Bid-Rigging," December 15.

Mainichi Daily News (1993b), "Kanemaru's Gone, but 'Dango' Continues to Thrive Under the Surface," May 4.

Mallen, Bruce (1973), "Functional Spin-Off: A Key to Anticipating Change in Distribution Structure," *Journal of Marketing*, 37 (July), pp. 18–25.

March, J. G. (1978), "Bounded Rationality, Ambiguity and the Engineering of Choice," *Bell Journal of Economics and Management Science*, 9 (Autumn), pp. 587–608.

Mason, Mark (1992), *American Multinationals and Japan: The Political Economy of Japanese Capital Control, 1899–1980*, Cambridge, Mass.: Harvard University Press.

Matsushita, Mitsuo (1987), "The Legal Framework of Japanese Industrial Policy," *Brigham Young University Law Review*, Vol. 1987, no.2, pp. 541–570.

Matsushita, Mitsuo (1990), *Introduction to Japanese Antimonopoly Law*, Tokyo: Yuhikaku Publishing.

Matsushita, Mitsuo (1991), "The Role of Competition Law and Policy in Reducing Trade Barriers in Japan," *World Economy*, 14, no.2 (June), pp. 181–197.

Matsushita, Mitsuo (1993), *International Trade and Competition Law in Japan*, Oxford, England: Oxford University Press.

McAnneny, Joseph W. (1991), "The Justice Department's Crusade Against Price Fixing: Initiative or Reaction?" *Antitrust Bulletin*, 36, no. 3 (Fall), pp. 521–542.

McGuinness, N. W., and B. Little (1981), "The Influence of Product Characteristics on the Export Performance of New Industrial Products," *Journal of Marketing*, 45 (Spring), pp. 110–122.

McKinney, Joseph A. (1989), "Degree of Access to the Japanese Market: 1979 vs. 1986," *Columbia Journal of World Business*, 24 no. 2 (Summer), pp. 53–59.

McWilliams, Abagail, and Dennis L. Smart (1993), "Efficiency v. Structure-Conduct-Performance: Implications for Strategy Research and Practice," *Journal of Management*, 19, no. 1, pp. 63–78.

Ministry of Foreign Affairs (1992), "The Role of Keiretsu in Business: Separating Facts from Fiction," a brochure printed by the Ministry of Foreign Affairs, Japan (January).

MITI (1992), *Naigai Kakaku Choosa Kekka ni Tsuite* (The Results of an Investigation of Foreign and Domestic Prices), Tokyo: Ministry of International Trade and Industry, April 26.

Montgomery, David B. (1991), "Understanding the Japanese as Customers, Competitors and Collaborators," *Japan and the World Economy*, 3, pp. 61–91.

Morimoto, Kokichi, ed. (1994), *Japan 1994: An International Comparison*, Keizai Koho Center, printed in Japan by Taiheisha, Ltd.

Mueller, Dennis C., and John E. Tilton (1969), "Research and Development Costs as a Barrier to Entry," *Canadian Journal of Economics*, 2 (November), pp. 570–579.

Murphy, William J. (1988), "Interfirm Cooperation in a Competitive Economic System," *American Business Law Journal*, 26, pp. 29–56.

Nakane, Chie (1970), *Japanese Society*, Berkeley: University of California Press.

Nakatani, Iwao (1984), "The Economic Role of Financial Corporate Grouping," in *The Economic Analysis of the Japanese Firm*, edited M. Aolei, Amsterdam: Elsevier Science Publishing, pp. 227–258.

Nakatani, Iwao (1992), *The Asymmetry of the Japanese-Style vs. American-Style Capitalism as the Fundamental Source of Japan-U.S. Imbalance Problems*, Tokyo, Japan: National Bureau of Economic Research and Japan Center for Economic Research.

Nakazawa, Toshiaki, and Leonard W. Weiss (1989), "The Legal Cartels of Japan," *Antitrust Bulletin*, 24 (Fall), pp. 641–653.

Neale, A. D., and M. L. Stephens (1988), *International Business and National Jurisdiction*, Oxford: Clarendon Press.

Neff, Robert (1989), "Rewriting the Book on How to Deal with Japan," *Business Week*, August 7, pp. 49.

Nelson, Philip B. (1991), "Reading Their Lips: Changes in Antitrust Policy Under the Bush Administration," *Antitrust Bulletin*, 26 (Fall), pp. 681–697.

Nikkei Weekly (1991), "Administrative Guidance Target of Bill," October 5.

Nikkei Weekly (1992), "MITI Seeking New Role for Itself in Mature Economy," May 30.

Nikkei Weekly (1993), "Guidelines Against Bid-Rigging Planned," October 10.

Nikkei Weekly (1994a), "Both Sides are to Blame for Collapse of Talks," February 28.

Nikkei Weekly (1994b), "Japan, U.S. Ready Reneging Data for Trade Talks," March 13.

Noland, Marcus (1991) "Export Targeting and Japanese Industrial Policy," in *Trade Theory and Economic Reform—North, South, and East: Essays in Honor of Bela Balassa*, edited by Jaime de Melo and Andre Sapir, Cambridge, Mass.: Basil Blackwell, pp. 183–200.

Noland, Marcus (1992), *Public Policies, Private Preferences, and Japan's Trade Pattern*, Washington, D.C.: Institute for International Economics (mimeographed, January).

Noland, Marcus (1993), "The Impact of Industrial Policy on Japan's Trade Specialization," *Review of Economics and Statistics*, 75, no. 2 (May), pp. 241–248.

Nye, Joseph S. (1992), "Coping with Japan," *Foreign Policy*, 89 (Winter), pp. 96–115.

OECD (1972), *The Industrial Policy of Japan*, Paris: Organization for Economic Cooperation and Development.

Ohlin, Bertil (1933), *Interregional and International Trade*, Cambridge, Mass.: Harvard University Press.

Ohmae, Kenichi (1982), *The Mind of the Strategist: The Art of Japanese Business*, New York: McGraw-Hill.

Okumura, Hiroshi (1990), "Unjustifiable Rationality of 'Keiretsu,'" *Ekonomisuto*, July 10.

Okuno-Fujiwara, Masahiro (1991), "Industrial Policy in Japan: A Political Economy View," in *Trade with Japan: Has the Door Opened Wider?* edited by Paul Krugman, Chicago: National Bureau of Economic Research, University of Chicago Press, pp. 271–303.

Ouchi, William (1980), "Markets, Bureaucracies, and Clans," *Administrative Science Quarterly*, 25 (March), pp. 129–141.

Ouchi, William (1981), *Theory Z: How American Business Can Meet the Japanese Challenge*, Boston, Mass.: Addison-Wesley.

Pascale, Richard T., and Anthony G. Athos (1981), *The Art of Japanese Management*, New York: Simon and Schuster.

Pempel, T. J. (1987), "The Unbundling of 'Japan, Inc.': The Changing Dynamics of Japanese Policy Formation," in *The Trade Crisis: How Will Japan Respond?*, edited by Kenneth B. Pyle, Seattle: Society for Japanese Studies, University of Washington.

Petri, Peter A. (1989), "Japanese Trade in Transition: Hypotheses and Recent Evidence," paper prepared for the National Bureau of Economic Research conference, The U.S. and Japan: Trade and Investment.

Phillips, Lynn W., Dae R. Chang, and Robert D. Buzzell (1983), "Product Quality, Cost Position and Business Performance: A Test of Some Key Hypotheses," *Journal of Marketing*, 47 (Spring), pp. 26–43.

Pickens, T. Boone (1991), "Foreign Investment in Japan: Keiretsu Business Practices," *Vital Speeches of the Day*, 57, no. 6 (January 1), pp. 171–172.

Porter, Michael E. (1978), "The Structure Within Industries and Companies' Performance," *Review of Economics and Statistics*, 61 (May), pp. 214–227.

Porter, Michael E. (1980a), *Competitive Strategy*, New York: Free Press.

Porter, Michael E. (1980b), "Industry Structure and Competitive Strategy: Keys to Profitability," *Financial Analysis Journal*, 36 (July-August), pp. 30–41.

Porter, Michael E. (1985), *Competitive Advantage: Creating and Sustaining Superior Performance*, New York: Macmillan.

Porter, Michael E., ed. (1986), *Competition in Global Industries*, Boston, Mass.: Harvard Business School Press.

Prahalad, C. K., and Gary Hamel (1990), "The Core Competence of the Corporation," *Harvard Business Review*, 68 (May-June), pp. 79–91.

Prescott, John E. (1986), "Environments as Moderators of the Relationship Between Strategy and Performance," *Academy of Management Journal*, 29, pp. 329–346.

Prestowitz, Clyde V., Jr. (1988a), "Japanese vs. Western Economics," *Technology Review*, May/June, pp. 27–36.

Prestowitz, Clyde V., Jr. (1988b), *Trading Places: How We Are Giving Our Future to Japan and How to Reclaim It*, New York: Basic Books.

Prestowitz, Clyde V., Jr. (1992), "In Search of Survival: Why Haven't We Done Anything?" *Vital Speeches of the Day*, 58, no. 22 (September 1), pp. 698–704.

Prestowitz, Clyde V., Jr., Lawrence Chimerine, and Paul Willen (1993), *Closing the Trade Gap with Japan*, Washington, D.C.: Economic Strategy Institute (mimeographed, November).

Rabino, Samuel (1980), "An Examination of Barriers to Exporting Encountered by Small Manufacturing Companies," *Management International Review*, 20, no. 1, pp. 67–73.

Ramseyer, J. Mark (1983), "Japanese Antitrust Enforcement After the Oil Embargo," *American Journal of Comparative Law*, 31, pp. 395–430.

Ramseyer, J. Mark (1985), "The Costs of the Consensual Myth: Antitrust Enforcement and Institutional Barriers to Litigation in Japan," *Yale Law Journal*, vol. 94, pp. 604–645.

Rapp, William V. (1986), "Japan's Invisible Barriers to Trade," in *Fragile Interdependence: Economic Issues in U.S.-Japan Trade and Investment*, edited by Thomas A. Pugel and Robert G. Hawkins, New York: Center for Japan-U.S. Business and Economics, New York University, pp. 21–62.

Richards, Jonathan D. (1993), "Japan Fair Trade Commission Guidelines Concerning Distribution Systems and Business Practices: An Illustration of Why Antitrust Law is a Weak Solution to U.S. Trade Problems with Japan," *Wisconsin Law Review*, May-June, pp. 921–960.

Robinson, Richard D., ed. (1987), *Direct Foreign Investment: Costs and Benefits*, New York: Praeger.

Rockwell, Keith M. (1989), "U.S. Firms Avoid Criticizing Japan," *Journal of Commerce*, December 19.

Rosson, Philip J., and L. David Ford (1982), "Manufacturer-Overseas Distributor Relations and Export Performance," *Journal of International Business Studies*, 13 (Fall), pp. 57–72.

Ruekert, Robert, Orville Walker, and Kenneth Roering (1985), "The Organization of Marketing Activities: A Contingency Theory Perspective," *Journal of Marketing*, (Winter), pp. 41–52.

Ryans, Adrian B. (1988), "Strategic Market Entry Factors and Market Share Achievement in Japan," *Journal of International Business Studies*, 19 (Fall), pp. 389–409.

Sakakibara, Eisuke (1992), "Japan: Capitalism Without Capitalists," *International Economic Insights*, 3, no. 4 (July/August), pp. 45–47.

Samiee, Saeed, and Kendall Roth (1992), "The Influence of Global Marketing Standardization on Performance," *Journal of Marketing*, 56 (April), pp. 1–17.

Sanekata, Kenji (1986), "Antitrust in Japan: Recent Trends and their Socio-Political Background," *University of British Columbia Law Review*, 20, no. 2, pp. 379–399.

Saso, Mary, and Stuart Kirby (1982), *Japanese Industrial Competition to 1990*, Cambridge, Mass.: Abt Books.

Saxonhouse, Gary R. (1983), "What Is All This About 'Industrial Targeting' in Japan?" *World Economy*, 6 (September), pp. 253–273.

Saxonhouse, Gary R. (1986), "Japan's Intractable Trade Surpluses in a New Era," *World Economy*, 9 (September), pp. 239–257.

Saxonhouse, Gary R. (1989), "Differentiated Products, Economies of Scale and Access to the Japanese Market," in *Trade Policies and International Competitiveness*, edited by Robert C. Feenstra, Cambridge, Mass.: National Bureau of Economic Research, pp. 145–174.

Saxonhouse, Gary R. (1991), Comment on "How Open is Japan?" by Robert Z. Lawrence, in *Trade with Japan: Has the Door Opened Wider?* edited by Paul Krugman, Chicago: National Bureau of Economic Research, University of Chicago Press, pp. 38–46.

Saxonhouse, Gary R. (1993), "Economic Growth and Trade Relations: Japanese Performance in Long-Term Perspective," in *Trade and Protectionism*, edited by Takatoshi Ito and Anne O. Krueger, Chicago, University of Chicago Press.

Scherer, F. M. (1970), *Industrial Market Structure and Economic Performance*, Chicago: Rand McNally.

Schultz, Charles (1987), "Industrial Policy: A Dissent," *Brookings Review*, 5 no. 1 (Fall), pp. 3–12.

Scott, Bruce R. (1989), "Competitiveness: Self-Help for a Worsening Problem," *Harvard Business Review*, 67 (July-August), pp. 115–121.

Second Annual Report of SII Follow-Up (1992), jointly published by the governments of Japan and the United States, July 30.

Sekiguchi, Sueo, and Toshihiro Horiuchi (1985), "Myth and Reality of Japan's Industrial Policies," *World Economy*, 8, no. 4 (December), pp. 373–391.

Shepherd, W. (1979), *The Economics of Industrial Organization*, Englewood Cliffs, N.J.: Prentice-Hall.

Shimaguchi, Mitsuaki, and William Lazer (1979), "Japanese Distribution Systems: Invisible Barriers to Market Entry," *MSU Business Topics*, 27 (Winter), pp. 49–62.

Shimizu, Yositake (1993), "Japan's Price of Prosperity," *Daily Yomiuri*, October 13.

Simmons, Andre (1962), *The Sherman Antitrust Act and Foreign Trade*, Gainesville: University of Florida Monographs, Social Sciences, no. 16 (Fall).

Slovic, Paul, Baruch Fischhoff, and Sarah Lichtenstein (1977), "Behavioral Decision Theory," *Annual Review of Psychology*, 28, pp. 1–39.

Smith, Lee (1990), "Fear and Loathing of Japan," *Fortune*, February 26, pp. 24–30.

Snyder, Edward A. (1989), "New Insights into the Decline of Antitrust Enforcement," *Contemporary Policy Issues*, 7 (October), pp. 1–18.

Snyder, Edward A. (1990), "The Effect of Higher Criminal Penalties on Antitrust Enforcement," *Journal of Law and Economics*, 33 (October), pp. 439–462.

Srinivasan, T. N. (1991), "Is Japan an Outlier Among Trading Countries?" in *Trade Theory and Economic Reform—North, South, and East: Essays in Honor of Bela Balassa*, edited by Jaime de Melo and Andre Sapir, Cambridge, Mass.: Basil Blackwell, pp. 163–182.

Staiger, Robert W., Alan V. Deardorff, and Robert M. Stern (1988), "The Effects of Protection on the Factor Content of Japanese and American Foreign Trade," *Review of Economics and Statistics*, 70, no. 3 (August), pp. 475–483.

Stern, Robert M. (1989), "Introduction," in *Trade and Investment Relations Among the United States, Canada, and Japan*, edited by Robert M. Stern, Chicago: University of Chicago Press.

Terutomo, Ozawa (1986), "Japanese Policy Toward Foreign Multinationals: Implications for Trade and Competitiveness," in *Fragile Interdependence: Economic Issues in U.S.-Japan Trade and Investment*, edited by Thomas A. Pugel and Robert G. Hawkins, New York: Center for Japan-U.S. Business and Economics, New York University.

Thomas, Robert J. (1989), "Patent Infringement of Innovations by Foreign Competitors: The Role of the U.S. International Trade Commission," *Journal of Marketing*, 53 (October), pp. 63–75.

Thorelli, Hans B., ed. (1977), *Strategy + Structure = Performance: The Strategic Planning Imperative*, Bloomington, Indiana University Press.

Tookey, D. A. (1964), "Factors Associated with Success in Exporting," *Journal of Management Studies*, 1 (March), pp. 48–66.

Totten, Bill (1992), "Don't Blame Japan," *Tokyo Report*, 17, no. 11 (December), p. 1.

Townsend, James B. (1980), *Extraterritorial Antitrust: The Sherman Antitrust Act and U.S. Business Abroad*, Boulder, Colo.: Westview Press.

Toyama, Kozo, Norifumi Tateishi, and John Palenberg (1983), "Trade Friction, Administrative Guidance and Antimonopoly Law in Japan," *Case Western Reserve Journal of International Law*, 15, pp. 601–610.

Trezise, Philip, and Yukio Suzuki (1976), "Politics, Government, and Economic Growth in Japan," in *Asia's New Giant*, edited by Hugh Patrick and Henry Rosovsky, Washington, D.C.: Brookings Institution.

Tyson, Laura D'Andrea (1989), Comment on "Differentiated Products, Economies of Scale, and Access to the Japanese Market," by Gary R. Saxonhouse in *Trade Policies and International Competitiveness*, edited by Robert C. Feenstra, Cambridge, Mass.: National Bureau of Economic Research, pp. 175–180.

Tyson, Laura D'Andrea and John Zysman (1989), "Developmental Strategy and Production Innovation in Japan," in *Politics and Productivity: The Real Story of Why Japan Works*, edited by Chalmers Johnson, Laura D'Andrea Tyson, and John Zysman, Cambridge, Mass.: Ballinger.

Uekusa, Masu (1987), "Industrial Organization: The 1970s to the Present," in *The Political Economy of Japan: The Domestic Transformation*, edited by Kozo Yamamura and Yasukichi Stanford, Calif.: Yasuba, Stanford University Press.

Uekusa, Masu (1990), "Government Regulations in Japan: Toward Their International Harmonization and Integration," in *Japan's Economic Structure: Should It Change?* edited by Kozo Yamamura, Society for Japanese Studies, Seattle: University of Washington, pp. 237–269.

Uesugi, Akinori (1986), "Japanese Antitrust Developments," *International Business Lawyer*, 14 (June), pp. 195–198.

U.S. Department of Commerce (1987), *The Export Trading Company Guidebook*, Washington, D.C.: International Trade Administration.

U.S. Department of Commerce (1991), *The Joint DOC/MITI Price Survey: Methodology and Results*, Washington, D.C.: U.S. Department of Commerce (December).

U.S. Department of Justice (1992), "Antitrust Division Workload Statistics for Fiscal Years 1983–1992," obtained through personal correspondence with the Department of Justice.

van Wolferen, Karel (1989), *The Enigma of Japanese Power: People and Politics in a Stateless Nation*, New York: Alfred A. Knopf.

Victor, A. Paul, and John G. Chou (1985), "U.S. Antitrust Jurisdiction over Overseas Disputes, After Title IV of the 1982 Trading Company Act, and *Timberlane*," in *Antitrust Laws and Interna-*

tional Trade, 25th Annual Advanced Antitrust Seminar, Donald I. Baker, Joshua F. Greenberg, and John J. Hanson, Chairmen, Practicing Law Institute, pp. 11–58.

Vogel, Ezra F. (1979), *As Number One: Lessons for America*, Cambridge, MA: Harvard University Press.

Waesche, Horst (1993), "Success in Japan," an address delivered to the Seminar '93 Regional Investment Opportunities in Japan, held at the Keidanren Kaikan, Tokyo, on March 4, 1993.

Wall Street Journal (1990), Letters to the Editor, March 20 (Asia edition).

Wall Street Journal (1993a), "Report Accuses 44 Nations of Unfair Trade Practices," April 1 (Asia edition).

Wall Street Journal (1993b), "Trade Data Don't Always Reflect Big Surplus from Service Exports," November 22 (Asia edition).

Wenders, John T. (1971), "Excess Capacity as an Entry Barrier," *Journal of Industrial Economics*, 20 (November), pp. 14–19.

Williamson, Oliver E. (1963), "Selling Expense as a Barrier to Entry," *Quarterly Journal of Economics*, 77 (February), pp. 112–128.

Williamson, Oliver E. (1979), "Transactions-Cost Economics: The Governance of Contractual Relations," *Journal of Law and Economics*, 22 (October), pp. 233–261.

Wind, Yoram (1986), "The Myth of Globalization," *Journal of Consumer Marketing*, 3 (Spring), pp. 23–26.

Yamamura, Kozo (1967), *Economic Policy in Postwar Japan: Growth versus Economic Democracy*, Berkeley and Los Angeles: University of California Press.

Yamamura, Kozo (1982), "Success that Soured: Administrative Guidance and Cartels in Japan," in *Policy and Trade Issues of the Japanese Economy: American and Japanese Perspectives*, edited by Kozo Yamamura, Seattle: University of Washington Press, pp. 77–112.

Yamamura, Kozo (1990), "Will Japan's Economic Structure Change? Confessions of a Former Optimist," in *Japan's Economic Structure: Should It Change?* edited by Kozo Yamamura, Seattle: Society for Japanese Studies, University of Washington, pp. 13–64.

Yang, Yoo S., Robert P. Leone, and Dana L. Alden (1992), "A Market Expansion Ability Approach to Identify Potential Exporters," *Journal of Marketing*, 56 (January), pp. 84–96.

Yomiuri Report from Japan (1994), "Daiei Chief Complains About Bureaucratic Delays," May 13.

Index

About the Authors

MASAAKI KOTABE is Professor of Marketing and International Business, Ambassador Edward Clark Centennial Fellow in Business, and also Director of Research at the Center for International Business Education and Research at the University of Texas at Austin. He is recognized by the *Journal of International Business Studies* as one of the most productive contributors to scholarly publications in international business in the past 25 years. He is also the author of *Global Sourcing Strategy: R&D, Manufacturing, Marketing Interfaces* (Quorum, 1992), *Japanese Distribution System* (1993), and *Marketing Management* (1996).

KENT W. WHEILER is Senior Analyst for Weyerhaeuser Company's pulp and paper complex in Longview, Washington. After completing his Ph.D. program in marketing at the University of Texas at Austin in 1987, he joined the market research group at Weyerhaeuser's Engineered Wood Products Division. From 1988 to 1994 he lived in Tokyo, Japan, as the Director of Finance and Administration for Weyerhaeuser Far East, Ltd., working throughout Asia supporting Weyerhaeuser's $1 billion-plus business in the region. Prior to his doctoral studies, he worked for Arthur Andersen & Co. as an auditor, where he qualified as a certified public accountant (CPA) in 1983.

ISBN 0-275-95628-8

90000>

HARDCOVER BAR CODE